Henry Charles Carey

Reconstruction: Industrial, Financial, and Political

Letters to the Hon. Henry Wilson, U. S. Senator from Massachusetts

Henry Charles Carey

Reconstruction: Industrial, Financial, and Political
Letters to the Hon. Henry Wilson, U. S. Senator from Massachusetts

ISBN/EAN: 9783337133856

Printed in Europe, USA, Canada, Australia, Japan

Cover: Foto ©ninafisch / pixelio.de

More available books at **www.hansebooks.com**

RECONSTRUCTION:

INDUSTRIAL, FINANCIAL, AND POLITICAL.

LETTERS

TO THE

HON. HENRY WILSON,

U. S. SENATOR FROM MASSACHUSETTS.

BY

HENRY C. CAREY.

PUBLISHED BY
THE UNITED PRESS ASSOCIATION,
WASHINGTON.
1868.

LETTERS TO THE HON. HENRY WILSON,

SENATOR FROM MASSACHUSETTS.

LETTER FIRST.

DEAR SIR:

In the recent Address at Saratoga your hearers were told that you were "accustomed to take hopeful views of public affairs;" that "during the darkest hours of the war" you had had "faith in the country, faith in our democratic institutions," and had "never doubted the result;" that, "since the close of the war," we had had "trials quite as severe," but you had "never had any doubt" that that result was "to be a great and united nation." Continuing on in the same direction, you spoke as follows:—

"We have passed through a bloody struggle. I am among those who believe that it was inevitable—that it was one of the great wars of the human family. It was a struggle on this continent between the democratic ideas of the Declaration of Independence and the system of human bondage, and in such a contest there could be no doubt of the result. We who stood by our country, and the cause of liberty, justice, and humanity, have triumphed. We have triumphed at a fearful cost. We are proud and strong; we have lifted the country toward the heavens; we are a greater people than ever before. We have destroyed human bondage; we have subjugated and conquered a brave and heroic portion of the country, and now the great work is done, I am for welcoming them back with warm and generous greetings, trusting that the causes of all our troubles have passed away forever, and that hereafter in the future we shall be friends and brothers as we were in the morning of the Republic."

The anticipations here presented are most pleasant and agreeable, and gladly would I accept them as likely to be realized were it possible for me so to do. That I do not, is due to the plain and simple fact that sad experience is now teaching the farming and mining States that for them the only "result" thus far recently achieved has been that of a change of masters, Massachusetts having, so far as regards material interests generally, taken the place of South Carolina, and New England at large, in reference to some of high importance, that of the States so recently in rebellion. Power has gone from the extreme South to the extreme North, and the sectionalism of to-day is likely, as I think, to prove quite as injurious as has already proved that of the past.

This, I pray you, my dear sir, to believe, is said in no unfriendly spirit. No one more than I respects the great mass of the people of Massachusetts. Few have given more full expression to their admiration of the estimable qualities by which New England people generally are so much distinguished. It is because of my respect for them, because of my desire for their continued happiness and prosperity, that I desire now, through you, to ask consideration of the facts, that they now exercise a political power wholly disproportioned to their numbers; that the State in which I reside, with *two* Senators, has a population nearly equal to that of New England with *twelve* Senators; that, as a consequence, the Senate, as regards economical questions generally, is now in frequent conflict with the House; that the day is at hand when there will be a dozen States, each one of which will outnumber all New England; that abolition of slavery has removed the difficulties which so long had stood in the way of union between the Centre and the South; that of all the States there are none that, for that reason, should so studiously as your own avoid suspicion of improper use of power; that to enable the East to maintain its present political position there is needed a most discreet, most careful, most magnanimous exercise thereof; and that, for want of that care, for want of that discretion, for want of that magnanimity, the Union is to-day, in my belief, more endangered than it had been in the years by which the war had been immediately preceded.

That you will *now* believe this I do not at all expect. Neither did I expect Mr. Dallas to believe me when, less than ten years since, in answer to a question as to when the Capitol would be completed, I told him that it would be "just about the time when the Union would be dissolved." "Nothing," as I then added, "could stand against a system which, like that of the tariff of 1846, made Liverpool the centre of exchange among ourselves and with the world at large, and made of our railroads mere conduits to be used for carrying to Britain the soil of the country in the form of wheat, corn, tobacco, and cotton. It would," as I continued, "ruin any country of the world." Of this he did not *then* believe a single word. Nevertheless, two years afterwards, when *too late*, he did believe it. So, as I fear, will it be with your constituents and yourself. They will believe nothing of the danger until the ruin shall have come, as, without a change of policy, come it must, and before the close of the next decade.

An enlightened foreigner, one who had had abundant opportunities for studying our people, said of them, but a few years since, that "none so soon forgot yesterday." Nothing was ever more truly said. Rarely, if ever, do we study the past. We never, in any manner, in our public affairs, profit by experience, whether our own or that of others. Be the question before us what it may, great or small, it is treated precisely as if none such had, here or elsewhere, ever before arisen; and hence it is that our movements so much resemble those of a blind giant, daily forced to look for advice to the one-eyed dwarfs by whom we are surrounded. Were it otherwise—could our people, North and South, East and West, but be persuaded to study a very little of *their own* history—could it, do you think, be made to pay for Britain to employ so many of her people, Irish and English, Christian and Hebrew, in the work of teaching them the advantage to be derived from maintaining and increasing their dependence upon a country whose movements were becoming daily more irregular and uncertain; whose power for self direction was diminishing with each succeeding year; one that to-day had not, outside of this Union, a friend on earth; one that had already passed its zenith, and for the reason that the societary ruin by which she was surrounded was in the direct ratio of the reliance of others on her friendship? Seeking evidence of this, let me beg you to look to Ireland, the land of "popular famines;" to Turkey, with which she has for centuries been in close free trade alliance; to Portugal, once the most valuable of her customers; to India, in which the millions who formerly were occupied in the cotton manufacture, are now "festering in compulsory idleness;" to China, brought to a state of anarchy by means of wars made for maintaining the illicit opium trade; to Japan, likely, according to Earl Grey, soon to be reduced to the condition in which China now exists; to Australia, now little more than a great sheep walk, whose occupants, in default of any market for their products, are now again converting their flocks into tallow; to New Brunswick and Nova Scotia, both abounding in coal and ores, while compelled to import all the iron they use; and finally, to Canada, whose population has for the past few years been steadily passing to the land of the stars and stripes, seeking there the *protection* denied to them at home. Look where you may, you will find prosperity to exist *in the inverse ratio of the connection with Britain.* Look even to France and see that loss of position before the world has gone hand in hand with her adoption of the British system. Seeking evidence of these decaying tendencies, you may with advantage turn to the last *Edinburgh Review,* finding therein a proposition for military alliance between the two countries as the only mode of preventing further loss of caste.

Britain has been long engaged in building an inverted pyramid; but at no period has her progress in that direction been so rapid as within the last twenty years, the free trade period. The important class of small landholders so much admired by Adam Smith—that class which so long had constituted the right arm of British strength—has now almost entirely disappeared, half of the land of England being owned by 150 men, and half of that of Scotland by a single dozen. So, too, is it in regard to all industrial pursuits, a perpetual series of crises having crushed out the smaller and more useful men, and all the processes of mining and manufacture having passed into the hands of the few whose vast fortunes had enabled them to profit by the ruin of the lesser men by whom they had been surrounded. In consequence of this it is, that British society daily more and more exhibits the phenomena of squalid poverty side by side with enormous wealth; precisely the state of things that, under the free trade and pro-slavery policy, had, before the war, obtained throughout the Cotton States. To these latter it brought the weakness that has recently been so well exhibited. To the former it has brought the decay of influence that has, on a recent occasion, led a reflecting British writer to say to his countrymen that "the counsels which Lord Stanley is said to be pressing both at Berlin and Paris, count for about as much as if they came from the cabinet of Sweden or Portugal;" than which nothing could be more true—Britain having no longer a place in the European system. To enable her to maintain a place anywhere she must break up this Union, and to the consciousness of this has been due the fact that, with the exception of the mere laboring class, nearly the whole body of the British people has exhibited itself before the world as advocate of a system which has human slavery for its corner-stone, and as ready to make any sacrifice of honor or of conscience, public or private, that might be needed for securing its permanent establishment. Thus far she has failed; but, having now before her only the choice between, on the one hand, the disruption of our Union, and, on the other, her own descent from the position she so long has occupied, we may be quite assured that no effort will be spared that may seem to tend towards accomplishment of the former.

To prevent this would be an easy task could our people but be persuaded to study a very little of the past, with a view to an understanding of the present, and to preparation for the future. That you at least, my dear sir, may be induced so to do, I propose in another letter to present for your consideration a brief view of the mode by which preparation had before the war been made for accomplishment of the ruin from which we so recently have escaped, meantime remaining, with great regard,

Yours, truly,

HENRY C. CAREY.

Hon. HENRY WILSON.

PHILADELPHIA, Aug. 20, 1867.

LETTER SECOND.

Dear Sir :—

Before prescribing for removal of fever the skilful physician seeks to ascertain why it exists, varying his treatment with variation in the cause discovered. The quack treats all fevers alike, and kills his patients. What is true with regard to physical evil is equally so with reference to social disease, it being essential that we understand the ultimate cause of error before we write the prescription for its cure. In the case now before us you charge all our recent troubles to the existence of slavery, but your Address furnishes no answer to the previous question, *Why had it been that slavery had so rapidly grown in power?* Studying the matter more carefully you will, I think, find that, like the fever, slavery had been the mere symptom, and that if you would now prevent its recurrence, if you would really and permanently establish human freedom, you must begin by eradicating the cause, just as you would remove trouble of the head by treatment of the stomach. In no other way can permanent reconstruction be secured. Of that you may rest assured.

That you, my dear sir, may arrive at a proper understanding of the ultimate cause of our recent troubles, look around you in Massachusetts and satisfy yourself that it has been precisely as pursuits have been more and more diversified, *precisely as competition for the purchase of labor has increased,* that the weak have been rising to a level with the strong, that the woman has been coming more near to an equality with the man, the man himself more and more acquiring the power of self-direction. Look again, and see that diversification of employment has always grown most rapidly in periods of protection against the working of the British monopoly system, and that then it has always been that the capitalist has been obliged to seek the laborer. Look then further, and see that it has been in periods of British free trade, so-called, but really monopoly, that the laborer has lost the power of self-direction and has been obliged to seek the capitalist, and then determine for yourself which has in the North proved the road to freedom.

Turn next south, and see that slavery had grown in power just as the land had become more and more monopolized, as the little proprietors more and more disappeared from the stage, as the laborer everywhere found himself more and more compelled to limit himself to the single pursuit of raising raw material for the supply of distant markets, the proper work of the barbarian and the slave, and of those alone. That done, you will, as I think, better understand why it has been that freedom had tended upward in all that portion of the country that had accepted the idea of protection, and downward in those that had resisted it. There is but one road to freedom, peace, and harmony, and that is found in such diversification of pursuits as leads to enlargement of domestic commerce, and stimulation of the societary circulation.

British policy looks to arrest of the circulation of the world by means of compelling all raw material produced to pass through its little workshop. It is a monopoly system, and therefore it is that poverty, disease, and famine, all of which unite for the production of slavery, are chronic diseases in every country wholly subjected to British influence.

Therefore, too, has it been that British agents have been always in such close alliance with the slave-holding aristocracy of the South; and that, throughout the late war, British public opinion has been so nearly universally on the side of the men who have publicly proclaimed that slavery was to be regarded as the proper corner-stone of all free institutions.

British free trade, industrial monopoly, and human slavery, travel together, and the man who undertakes the work of reconstruction without having first satisfied himself that such is certainly the fact, will find that he has been building on shifting sands, and must fail to produce an edifice that will be permanent. So believing, and seeing in your Address nothing that indicates a proper appreciation of the fact that it is to a diversification of our pursuits, *alone*, we are to look for permanent establishment of human freedom and national independence, for permanent reconstruction of the Union, I am led to ask you to accompany me in an examination of the real causes of the rebellion that is proposed now to make. Let these be ascertained, and you may then safely proceed in the great work in which you are so actively engaged, but not before. Without this you will be prescribing for permanent dissolution, and not for reconstruction.

Within the last half century, compelled thereto by the general ruin that has in each and every case resulted from permitting the advocates of pro-slavery and British monopoly ideas to dictate our course of action, we have three times sought to establish domestic commerce and thus to achieve a real independence. In each of these the country almost at once revived, commerce became active, labor came again into demand, and prosperity reigned throughout the land. Throughout each and every of them, however, British money has been lavishly applied to the work of teaching the vast advantage to be derived from coming again under the British yoke; from again submitting to be compelled to make all our exchanges with the world at large in a single, distant, and diminutive market; and from thus uniting with British traders in the work of preventing the growth of human freedom. As a consequence of these teachings, and of the constant stimulation in that direction by the advocates of human slavery as it existed in this western world, the tariffs of 1828 and 1842 were allowed an existence of less than five years each, the general result having been, that of the last five and forty years by which the war had been preceded, there had been less than ten in which our policy had tended in the direction of human freedom and national independence.

Brief as had been the existence of the first of these tariffs its close found the country so far advanced in the right direction that the foreign debt, public and private, had been entirely discharged. Nevertheless, but seven years of the then re-established British monopoly system with its perpetually-recurring financial crises; its destruction of internal commerce; its annihilation of confidence; and its paralyzing effects in destroying the demand for labor; sufficed for plunging the country more deeply in debt than it ever before had been, and for making us more than ever dependent upon the chances and changes of a market that, more than any other, is governed by men who find their advantage in bringing about those sudden upward and downward movements by means of which they are themselves enriched, their humble dependents throughout the world being meanwhile ruined. The end in view is *trading despotism*, of all despotisms the most degrading to the unfortunate beings subjected to it. The name by which it is generally known is that of *British free-trade*—a freedom that carries with it slavery in the various forms of war, poverty, famine, and pestilence, and for emancipation from which, as has so well been proved in Ireland, its unfortunate subjects can find but a single road—that one which terminates at the grave. Of all, it is the meanest, most selfish, most soul-destroying; yet are its advocates among ourselves found among those who most profess a belief in human freedom.

Under the tariff of 1842 we resumed the road towards independence, commencing discharge of the heavy obligations incurred in the seven years of the monopoly system, and so rapid was our progress in that direction that but a single decade would have been required for the attainment of perfect emancipation. That, however, did not suit the admirers of, and believers in, human slavery, either at home or abroad. The system was to be broken down, and to that end our farmers were assured that if they would but consent to re-establish Liverpool in its old position of centre of the Union, at which the farmer of Illinois should make all his exchanges with his neighbor of Tennessee, our grain exports would speedily count by hundreds, if not even by thousands, of millions of dollars. The ridiculous absurdity of all such calculations now exhibits itself in the fact, that our average export to Britain of wheat and flour, for the last ten years, has been but the equivalent of little more than 10,000,000 cwts., or 16,000,000 bushels. It is, however, the business of British agents—that for which they are so well paid—to deceive and cheat our people. Should you desire new evidence to this effect, look, I pray you, to the fact, that the British Free-Trade League, which holds its meetings in New York, and which is supported by contributions of British traders, has just now refused the offer of their American opponents to institute a free discussion, by means of which all might be enabled to see both sides of the question. No journal in foreign pay ever, by any chance, permits its subscribers to see the argument in favor of industrial independence. No *American* journalist would hesitate for a moment to enter into any arrangement by means of which all should be enabled to see the argument *pro* and *con* on this important subject.

From the date of the re-establishment in 1846 of the British monopoly system we went steadily forward destroying the domestic commerce, increasing our dependence on Liverpool as a place of exchange with all the world, and augmenting our foreign debt, until all at once the inevitable result was reached—that of dissolution of the Union. That no other could have been arrived at will, as I think, be clearly obvious to you when you shall have studied the facts that will now be given.

Under the free-trade system, with its constantly increasing dependence on the most unstable and irregular market of the world, proper development of the abounding mineral wealth of the Central States was entirely impossible. As a consequence of this, nearly the whole increase of Northern population was forced to seek the prairie lands of the Northwest and West, there to employ themselves in tearing out the soil and exporting it, in the form of wheat or corn, to markets of the East, home or foreign; and thus, as far as in their power lay, increasing competition for *the sale* of food, and of all other raw materials they had to sell, while increasing competition for *the purchase* of iron, and all the commodities they had need to buy—that being the especial object of the monopoly system established by Britain, and now given to the world as tending to the promotion of freedom of commerce. As a further consequence, the Slave States of the Centre, unable to develop and mine their numerous and abounding ores, were compelled to send their people south; and thus did we, from day to day, increase the weight and power of the *extreme North* and the *extreme South*, while depopulating and weakening the Centre.

That you may fully understand the effects of this, and how it had been that secession had gradually become not only possible but inevitable, I pray you now to take up a railroad map of the Union, and mark the fact that *all our great roads are merely spokes of a wheel whose hub is found in Liverpool.* Those of them which have most tended to acquire strength and weight are those which have found their terminations north of Pennsylvania, and south of Virginia. With each and every stage of movement in that direction it became more and more impracticable that the two extremes could hold together, until at length they parted company in 1861. That such was the tendency of the British monopoly system, and that such must certainly be the result, had long been clearly obvious to me, when, less than ten years since, I told Mr. Dallas, then in London, that dissolution of the Union would come about the time when the Capitol should be completed. In this I erred, the building being not even yet quite finished. Whether or not, when it shall be so, it will be the Capitol of all the existing States, is very doubtful. Without a decided change of policy *it certainly will not*, the centrifugal force of the system now advocated by Massachusetts being too great to defy resistance.

What is it, my dear sir, that now so closely binds together the New England States? Is it not their *network* of roads. Could they now by any possibility be torn asunder? Certainly not. Could there be any difficulty in accomplishing this were there but two great parallel roads leading through Boston and Portland to Liverpool? Not in the least. Sectionalism would then be as rife in New England as it has been throughout the extreme south and extreme north. Mr. Lincoln saw clearly that the Mississippi was the cross-tie that had held the Union together, and therefore did he urge the making of another through the hills, recommending a road that should pass through Kentucky and East Tennessee. Congress refused the little aid that had been asked for, yet did it never hesitate at granting enormous quantities of land in aid of roads across the continent. So long as our legislation on all economic subjects shall continue to be sectional in its tendencies it is wholly vain to hope for permanent reconstruction. Had Mr. Lincoln's advice been taken, Kentucky would now, in all probability, be a republican State.

Having thus shown the sectional and pro-slavery tendencies of the British monopoly system, I propose now to ask your attention to the manner in which *construction* has been elsewhere accomplished, believing that when this shall have been properly understood there will be less difficulty about measures of *reconstruction*.

I remain yours, &c.,

HENRY C. CAREY.

Hon. Henry Wilson.

Philadelphia, Aug., 1867.

LETTER THIRD.

DEAR SIR:

Ten years since I expressed the belief that Germany, whose " national sin for the last two centuries," according to Chevalier Bunsen, " had been poverty, the condition of all classes, with few exceptions"—Germany, which thirty years before had been held to be immensely overpopulated—then already stood "first in Europe in point of intellectual development," and was " advancing in the physical and moral condition of her people with a rapidity exceeding that of any other portion of the Eastern hemisphere."

Since then, an empire has been constructed embracing a population little short of 40,000,000, among whom education is universal; with a system of communications not excelled by that of any other country, with the exception of those provided for the very dense populations and limited territories of England and of Belgium; with an internal commerce as perfectly organized as any in the world, and growing from day to day with extraordinary rapidity ; with a market on the land for nearly all its products, and, as a necessary consequence, with an agricultural population that grows daily in both intelligence and power; with a mercantile marine that now numbers more than 10,000 vessels ; with a public treasury so well provided that not only has the late war left no debt behind, but that it has been at once enabled to make large additions to the provision for public education ;* and with private treasuries so well supplied as to enable her people not only with their own means to build their own furnaces and factories and construct their own roads, but also to furnish hundreds of millions to the improvident people of America, to be by them applied to the making of roads in a country the abundance of whose natural resources should long since have placed it in the position of money lender, rather than that now occupied of general money borrower.

The course of things on the two sides of the Atlantic has thus, as we see, been entirely different. On the one side there has been

---

* "Shocked as the Chamber was at the extent of the Budget, yet the Liberal party received with applause the announcement that a half million thalers was expended in order to increase the salaries of the teachers in the public schools. 200,000 thalers were devoted especially to the teachers of primary schools, a small sum, it will be said, for the teachers of a nation of twenty millions ; but the sum, in relation to the end proposed, is not so small as it at first sight seems. The primary schools are exclusively connected with the communities, and must be tolerably well maintained by the latter. And this sum is appropriated only to those communities which are too poor to pay the teachers sufficiently."—*Tribune Correspondence.*

a quiet and peaceful movement that has ended in *construction*. On the other a constant series of feuds, that has resulted in a need for *reconstruction*. Why it is that results so widely different have been obtained I propose now to show you.

Five and thirty years since, Germany and the American Union exhibited states of things directly antagonistic, the one to the other. The first was divided and disturbed, its internal commerce in every way embarrassed, its people and its various governments very poor, and with little hope in the future except that which resulted from the fact that negotiations were then on foot for the formation of a Customs Union, which shortly after was accomplished. In the other everything was different, the internal commerce having been more active than had ever before been known, the public treasury filled to overflowing, the national debt on the eve of extinction, and capital so much abounding as to make demand, for the opening of mines, the building of houses and mills, and the construction of roads, for all the labor power of a people that then numbered thirteen millions.

The cause of these remarkable differences was to be found in the facts, that, up to that time, Germany had wholly failed to adopt such measures of co-ordination as were needed for establishing rapidity of circulation among the 30,000,000, of which her society was then composed; whereas Congress had, four years before, and for the first time, adopted measures having for their object development of all the powers, physical, mental, or moral, of its population, all the wealth of its soil, and all the wonderful mineral deposits by which that soil was known to be underlaid. The one had failed to bring together the producer and consumer of food and wool, and had remained dependent upon traders in distant markets. The other had decided that such dependence should, at no distant time, come to an end; that producers and consumers should be brought together; and there had thence already resulted an activity of circulation and an improvement in physical and moral condition, the like of which had never before been known to be accomplished in so brief a period.

Three years later (1835), the two countries are once again found totally opposed, Germany having adopted the American system and thus provided for freedom of internal commerce, America simultaneously adopting that which to Germany had proved so utterly disastrous, and which had been then rejected. Thenceforth the one moved steadily forward in the direction of creating a great domestic commerce, doing this by means of a railroad system which should so bind together her whole people as to forbid the idea of future separation. The result already exhibits itself in the quiet creation of a powerful empire. The other meanwhile has constructed great roads by means of which it has been enabled to export its soil, in the forms of tobacco, corn, and cotton, to distant markets, and thus to destroy the power to maintain internal commerce—the result obtained exhibiting itself in a great rebellion that has cost the country, North and South, half a million of lives, the crippling of hundreds of thousands of men, and an expenditure of more thousands of millions than, properly applied, would have doubled the incomes of its whole people, while making such demand for human force, mental, moral, and physical, as would, in a brief period, have secured the establishment of universal freedom, with benefit to all, white and black, landowner and laborer. Such have been the widely different results of two systems of public policy, the one of which looks to introducing into society that proper, orderly arrangement which is found in every well-conducted private establishment, and by means of which each and every person employed is enabled to find the place for which nature had intended him; the other, meanwhile, in accordance with the doctrine of *laisser faire*, requiring that government should abdicate the performance of its proper duties, wholly overlooking the fact that the communities by which such teachings are carried into practical effect—those whose dependence on Britain is a growing one—now exhibit themselves before the world in a state of utter ruin.

Turn now, if you please, to a railroad map of Germany, and see how wide is the difference between it and a similar map of the Union. Instead of a few great railroad lines leading out of the country, and having for their objects the *compulsion* of the people of close adjoining States to go abroad to make exchanges—Tennessee and Alabama going to Manchester and Liverpool to exchange with their neighbors of Indiana and Illinois—you find a perfect network, by means of which every town throughout the whole extent of the new empire is enabled peacefully and cheaply to exchange with each and every other. Look again to the journals of the day, and see that it has been just now determined that every town of 1500 inhabitants shall at once be put into telegraphic communication with each and every other. Turn then your eyes homeward, and see that while Congress has been willing to grant aid to telegraphic communication *outside* of the Union, it has never, so far as I can recollect, been willing to do anything *inside* of it. That domestic commerce by means of which the most powerful empire of Europe has been constructed, and in little more than a quarter of a century, is here considered wholly unworthy of Congressional notice.

The difference between the two countries consists in this, that the one has been making a piece of cloth, warp and woof, all the parts of which become more firmly knitted together from day to day; the other, meanwhile, having made nothing but warp, the filling having been forgotten. The strength of the one has been recently strikingly manifested in the determination of Southern Germany, in defiance of French interference, to adhere anew to the Zollverein.* The weakness of the other now manifests itself

* "The leaders of the ' South German national party' in Bavaria, Wurtemburg, Baden, and Hesse-Darmstadt, have decided to hold a meeting at

in the necessity for interference, on the part of Massachusetts, with the internal affairs of Texas and Louisiana. With our eyes always directed to Liverpool our whole policy is made sectional, and not national, and until it shall be changed it is as certain as that light follows the rising of the sun, that there can be no permanent reconstruction.

The great backbone of the Union is found in the ridge of mountains which commences in Alabama, but little distant from the Gulf of Mexico, and extends northward, wholly separating the people who inhabit the low lands of the Atlantic slope from those who occupy such lands in the Mississippi valley, and its constituting a great free-soil wedge with its attendant free atmosphere, created by nature herself in the very heart of slavery, and requiring but a slight increase of size and strength to enable its inhabitants to control the southern policy, and thus to bring the entire South into perfect harmony with the North and West, and with the world at large. That you may fully satisfy yourself on this head, I ask you to take the map and pass your eye down the Alleghany ridge, flanked as it is by the Cumberland range on the west, and by that of the Blue Mountains on the east, giving in the very heart of the South itself a country larger than all Great Britain, in which the finest of climates is found in connection with land abounding in coal, salt, limestone, iron ore, gold, and almost every other material required for the development of a varied industry and for securing the highest degree of agricultural wealth; and then to reflect that it is a region which must necessarily be occupied by men who with their own hands till their own land, and one in which slavery could never by any possibility have more than a slight and transitory existence. That done, I ask you to determine whether or not I am right in the assertion that the South is clearly divided into three separate portions, two of which have desired to move in the direction of perpetual human slavery, while the third, inserted between them, has been, and is, by the force of circumstances, necessarily impelled towards freedom.

Admitting now that the policy of '42 had been maintained; that rapid circulation had made such demand for labor as to cause the annual importation of miners and laborers to count by hundreds of thousands, if not almost by millions; that all the wonderful min-

Stuttgart in the beginning of August, with the object of forming a league, in conjunction with the Prussian liberals, for achieving the unification of Germany. This decision is supposed, on good authority, to have been precipitated by overtures lately made by France at Carlsruhe, Munich, and Darmstadt, with the object of preventing the acceptance by the South German States of the Prussian proposals for a restoration of the Zollverein. These overtures, it is said, were made in a very dictatorial tone. The conduct of the French diplomatic agents in this matter has greatly provoked the South German Liberals, and has produced so strong a feeling against France in the South German States that even the Ultramontanes no longer venture to continue their advocacy of a French alliance against Prussia."

eral resources of the country above described had been placed in course of development; that roads had been made by means of which Cincinnati and Savannah, St. Louis and Charleston, Boston and Mobile, had been enabled freely to exchange together; that the country south had been gradually creating a network of roads, by means of which coal and iron miners, farmers and weavers, had been enabled to exchange their products; admitting, I say, all these things, would not the wealth and strength of the people of the hills have, long since, so far outweighed those of the men of the flats, as to enable the former to control and direct the movements of the States? Would not that domestic commerce have given us freedom for the negro, harmony and peace among the people, and love for the Union among the States? Would it, under such circumstances, have been possible to *drive* the southern people into secession? That it would not, you can scarcely, as I think, fail to admit. Whensoever we shall have a fixed policy, tending gradually towards giving to our whole people such a network of roads as now knits together the New England States; whensoever there shall be real freedom of trade between Georgia and Illinois, Carolina and Iowa; whensoever the people of the interior generally shall be enabled to prosper under a system which stimulates domestic competition for the *purchase* of all they have to sell, and for the *sale* of all they need to consume; then, but not till then, will the freedom of the so recently emancipated slave become something more than a mere form of words; and then, but not till then, will there be good reason, my dear sir, for believing in the realization of your agreeable anticipations.

Slavery *did not* make the rebellion. British free trade gave us sectionalism, and promoted the growth of slavery, and thus led to rebellion. Had Mr. Clay been elected in 1844, all the horrors of the past few years would have been avoided. Why was he not? Because free-trade stump orators of New York and Massachusetts, professing to be opposed to slavery, could not believe him radical enough to suit their purposes. They, therefore, gave us Messrs. Polk and Dallas, and by so doing precipitated the rebellion, for the horrors and the waste of which, North and South, they are largely responsible before both God and man. Judging, however, from recent letters and speeches, they are now willing to take the responsibility of the next secession movement, giving us at one moment the extremest anti-slavery doctrines, while at the next advocating that British free trade policy which had always commanded the approbation of southern slaveholders, and which has reduced, or is reducing, to a condition closely akin to slavery, the people of every community that has been, or is, subjected to it. Unable to see that any system based on the idea of cheapening the raw materials of manufactures, the rude products of agricultural and mining labor, tends necessarily to slavery, they make of themselves the pro-slavery men, *par excellence*, of the world.

To what extent the policy of your State has, since that time, been in accordance with the teachings of such men, I propose in another letter to examine, meanwhile, remaining

Yours faithfully,

HENRY C. CAREY.

Hon. H. Wilson.

Philadelphia, Aug. 26, 1867.

LETTER FOURTH.

Dear Sir:—

Forty years since, at the date of the agitation for the passage of that protective tariff of 1828, by means of which the country became first emancipated from the control of foreign money-lenders, the people of Massachusetts, as represented in Congress, were full believers in the advantages of the British free-trade system. Fourteen years having elapsed, during one-half of which they had, under protection, enjoyed the advantages derived from a peaceful and most profitable extension of domestic commerce; the other half having, on the contrary, furnished a series of free-trade and pro-slavery crises, ending in almost universal bankruptcy, and in an exhaustion of the national credit so complete that, after having, in 1835, finally extinguished the public debt, it had just then been found impossible to borrow abroad even a single dollar; Messrs. Choate and Sprague, representing Massachusetts in the Senate, are found gladly co-operating with Archer of Virginia, and other enlightened Southern Whigs, in the passage of the act of 1842, under which the consumption of iron and of cottons was, in the short space of less than half-a-dozen years, almost trebled; the country, meanwhile, resuming payment of its foreign debt, and re-acquiring the credit which it had required but a similar period of British free-trade so entirely to annihilate.

The protection granted by the tariff of '42, full and complete as it was, enabled Massachusetts—and for the first time—to compete in foreign markets for the sale of cottons. It enabled, too, the South to engage in their manufacture; and so rapid had, in 1848, been its progress, that Mr. Rhett, of the *Charleston Mercury*, was thereby led to predict, in a letter to Mr. Abbott Lawrence, that before the lapse of another decade, it would have ceased to export raw cotton. The prediction was one not likely to be so early realized, but even its half realization would have spared us all the cost in life, limb, and property, of the late rebellion, while it would so far have advanced the slave towards freedom as to have

2

relieved the existing Congress from all the necessity for those measures of reconstruction of which you speak, and in which you have been, and are, so actively engaged.

The repeal of the act of 1846 was followed by a political revolution which placed General Taylor in the Presidential chair, and gave, or seemed to give, to the friends of American labor, and American interests generally, power for re-establishing protection. Forthwith a convention was held at Newport for the purpose of deciding what it was that needed to be asked for. The result of its deliberations was given to me a fortnight later by the then recognized head of the cotton interest of your State, in the few brief words: "We do not desire any protection that will stimulate domestic competition." To put this into other words, it was to say:—

"We do not wish that the South or West should engage in manufactures, for that would make competition for the *purchase* of cotton, and raise the price of the raw material."

"We do not desire that the South or West should become manufacturers, for that would produce competition for the *sale* of cloth, and reduce our profits."

"The tariff of 1846 having already closed the few mills of the Centre and the South, we do not desire any tariff that could have the effect of reopening them, or of causing new ones to be erected."

"That tariff having broken down our competitors, has given us a monopoly, and we desire to keep it. Nevertheless, we desire to have the duties increased some five or ten per cent., for that would benefit us, and would not suffice for producing domestic competition either for purchase of the raw material, or for the sale of finished goods."

It was a very narrow view of the question, wholly rejecting, as it did, the idea of any harmony between the interests of the producers and consumers of cotton. It was the right British idea, then first, as I think, naturalized in this country, and from that time forward, as I propose to show, made the rule of action of your representatives in both houses of Congress. It was the pro-slavery idea, common sense teaching that "raw materials" represent agricultural and mining labor, and, that whatever tends to increase competition for their sale, and thus to reduce their prices, tends directly to the subjugation of the laborer, black or white, to the will of those by whom his labor is directed. Wherever raw materials are low in price, man, be his color what it may, and whether found in Ireland or India, in Jamaica or Alabama, in Canada or Illinois, is little better than a slave, the only difference being in the form in which the master's whip presents itself for examination. The well-fed negroes of the South were, ten years since, less enslaved than were those Irish people so accurately described by Thackeray as "starving by millions." The Russian serf, paying *obrok* to his master, and comfortably supporting his wife and children on the proceeds of his labor, was far more master of his actions and himself than this day are the small remnant of those Pennsylvania miners that, in April, 1861, threw aside their tools and rushed to the nation's rescue, finding themselves, as they do, wholly without the employment by means of which they might be enabled to obtain better supplies of food and clothing. Competition for the purchase of labor *makes* men and women free. The ballot-box is useful as a means of *perpetuating* freedom. In your Address I find much in reference to this latter, but in regard to the former, and infinitely the most important, you are, as is much to be regretted, wholly silent.

The election of Mr. Cobb, in 1849, as Speaker of the House, threw the committees into the hands of the Democrats, and your manufacturers, as a consequence, wholly failed to obtain that small additional protection for which they so steadily had asked; just as much as, but no more than, would give security to themselves,· while not in any manner "stimulating domestic competition" for purchase of cotton, or for the sale of cloth.

At the next step we find a coalition between British iron-masters and a self-constituted committee of three, having for its active head an ex-member of Congress from Massachusetts, since then presiding officer in one of the Republican conventions. This committee was, for a commission, to procure repeal of all duties on railroad iron, and return of much of those already paid. The movement failed; but for three years the sword of Damocles was held over the heads of all those engaged in the production of coal and iron, and at a cost to the mining interests of the country at large greater than would now suffice for buying and paying for all the cotton and woollen mills of your State, and all the towns in which those mills are placed.

Two years later the East proposed to the West, that, as compensation for granting it free wool, free raw material, and pro-slavery economic policy generally, it would itself generously consent to sacrifice the interests of its late co-laborers of the mining centre—of that section to which alone it had been indebted for the triumph of Whig principles in 1848. The proposition, in the form of an amendment to the appropriation bill, was strongly advocated by a distinguished Massachusetts member, shortly afterwards raised to the speakership, and it finally passed the House. It was defeated in the Senate, having there, on the last day of the session, been talked to death; this, too, in defiance of all the efforts of Massachusetts manufacturers, and of the readiness by them manifested to buy, and *pay for*, the silence of those engaged in the patriotic work.*

The first of these periods had been given to the closing of

---

* Should conclusive evidence on this subject be desired, it can at any hour be supplied.

existing rolling-mills, and preventing the building of others. In the second, it was claimed that because the mills were idle that, for that reason, the work of destruction should be further carried forward.

Simultaneously with these operations came the Canada reciprocity scheme, having for its object the cheapening of all the raw materials of manufacture that could be obtained from the country beyond the Bay of Fundy and the St. Lawrence, barley, wool, wheat, and coal, included. Wholly misunderstood, it passed the House, and was on the eve of becoming a law by means of senatorial action when I myself, for the first time, opened the eyes of Mr. Clay and other leading senators to the injurious, and even destructive, tendencies of the measure. From that hour the case became so hopeless that, as I think, the bill never afterwards came up for consideration. The election of Mr. Pierce, and consequent return of the pro-slavery party to power, brought about a change, however; it having then become to the South most clearly obvious that for preventing annexation of the British Possessions there was but a single remedy—that of granting to the Provinces all the advantages of being in the Union, while requiring of their people the performance of none of the duties, the bearing of none of the burdens, of American citizens. Such was the true intent and meaning of the treaty that then was negotiated, and that was carried through the Senate by aid of the combined pro-slavery and trading States, Massachusetts and New York steadily uniting with Carolina for preventing any change in the period for which it was to endure, and unanimously recording their votes against limiting it to one, two, three, and so on to nine years. To force through the House a bill providing for carrying it into effect was now the difficulty. That the work was done all know, but of the character of the means resorted to for having it done, few know who have not had the advantage I have had of hearing it fully described by one of the most honored and honorable members of the House. As in the case of the amendment to the appropriation bill above referred to, it seemed to be held that "the end"—the cheapening of raw materials at whatsoever cost to the farmers, miners, and laborers of the Union—"sanctified the means;" and "sanctified" them even in the eyes of men who long had found their chief employment in lecturing their fellow-citizens on the unchristian character of American slavery, and on the necessity for giving freedom to the Southern producers of those raw materials in the cheapening of which they found themselves so steadily engaged.

That this had been from first to last a Boston measure, is, of course, well known to you, as you must have seen the circulars asking subscriptions for moneys to be paid to the men who had succeeded in placing Canadians in a position far better than that occupied by our own citizens.

Close upon this followed the nomination of General Fremont,

another British free-trade measure forced upon the States of the Centre by extremists of the North and East. In the course of the campaign the agents of British makers of cloth and iron were, on one occasion, greatly gratified by a speech made in front of the New York Exchange by a gentleman of Massachusetts, who, in his character of Speaker of the House, had, but a few months previously, appointed committees entirely satisfactory to that portion of the body which had had full belief in *American* free-trade, and in the idea that every step in the direction of diversified industry tended towards emancipation for the laborer, black and white, foreign and domestic.

Coming now to 1857, we find the Ways and Means Committee, by its chairman, Mr. Campbell, of Ohio, reporting a bill for reduction of the revenue, somewhat satisfactory to the people of the Centre and the West. Wholly changed by a senatorial pro-slavery committee, with Mr. Hunter, of Virginia, at its head, it was then advocated by yourself, my dear sir, in a speech in which occurs the following passage, to wit:—

"The people of New England, Mr. President, and especially of Massachusetts, are very extensively engaged in the manufacture of articles in which wool, hemp, flax, lead, tin, brass, and iron are largely consumed. It is for their interest that the duties on these articles should be merely nominal, or that they should be duty free."

The opposition to this pro-slavery and cheap raw material substitute of the Virginia senator was very vigorous, Mr. Seward taking therein a very decided part. So doubtful, at length, became its adoption, that its friends found it necessary to telegraph your colleague, Mr. Sumner, advising him that without his vote the friends of freedom for the American mining and agricultural laborer, and of independence for the American Union, would probably succeed in accomplishing its rejection. He came, then presenting himself for the first time in the session, still suffering under injuries caused by the attack of a Carolinian opponent of the doctrine of diversified interests; and he then and there united with Virginia, Carolina, and Mississippi in a vote, the true intent and meaning of which was, that the farmers, miners, and laborers of America, black and white, should, in all the future, be mere "hewers of wood and drawers of water" for Southern slaveholders and British and Eastern capitalists.

On more than one occasion I had said to your Colleague that while he had spoken much of freedom, his senatorial votes on industrial questions had thus far always been given on the pro-slavery side. Meeting him in Paris shortly after the one last above recorded, I could not refrain from congratulating him on having so far recovered from the effects of Carolinian brutality as to have been enabled to unite with Carolinian senators in a vote for perpetuation of slavery throughout the South. In the true Christian spirit he had returned good for evil.

The passage of that act brought about a crisis, whose effect was that of almost total stoppage of cotton and woollen mills throughout the country north and south. For the moment Massachusetts suffered some little inconvenience, but she soon after resumed operations, and with great advantage to herself, her rivals in the Central, Southern, and Western States having been irretrievably ruined. The danger of "domestic competition" had disappeared, and the manufacturing monopoly had become assured.

The years that followed exhibited an almost total prostration of the various industries of the country, yet was it determined by the leaders of the Republican party, North and East, that the platform to be adopted at Chicago should be a mere repetition of that of 1856, all "new issues" to be entirely ignored. On the Committee of Resolutions there was, however, one member who was determined that the question of protection should be squarely met, and he therefore notified his fellow-members that if they did not then and there adopt a resolution to that effect they should be compelled to fight it on the following day on the floor of the convention. In that he, representing New Jersey, was sustained by the member from Delaware, and the debate terminated by the adoption of a resolution in the following words, the reading of which, on the succeeding day, was followed by a storm of applause from the assembled thousands, the like of which has had no parallel on this Western Continent:—

" That, while providing revenue for the support of the General Government by duties upon imports, *sound policy requires such an adjustment of those imposts as to encourage the development of the industrial interests of the whole country;* and we commend that policy of national exchanges which secures to the workingmen liberal wages, to agriculture remunerating prices, to mechanics and manufacturers an adequate reward for their skill, labor, and enterprise, and to the nation commercial prosperity and independence."

Such is the history of the decade. It is the history of a constant war by Massachusetts upon the greatest of all the national interests—a war for sixpences, carried on at an annual cost to the mining and farming regions of the country five times greater than the receipts of California gold—a war more than half the cost of which was paid by Pennsylvania. To the Union at large its cost consists in this, that had Massachusetts fully, fairly, and honestly exerted her influence in the opposite direction, the iron manufacture of the Border States would probably have made such progress as to have prevented their secession, and thus prevented all the injury, as regards both property and life, they have been made to suffer.

Of what has since occurred I shall speak in another letter, meanwhile remaining,

Yours, very truly,

HENRY C. CAREY.

Hon. Henry Wilson.

LETTER FIFTH.

DEAR SIR:—

By the adoption, as part of its platform, of the resolution given in my last, the Republican party pledged itself to a policy the reverse of that advocated by yourself in 1857; one which looked to "stimulation of competition" for the purchase of raw materials, labor included; one which would "stimulate domestic competition" for the sale of finished commodities; one based on the idea, apparently unknown to our Massachusetts friends, that protection to the miner, by giving him means of purchase, is, in effect, protection to the maker of cloth; and that protection to consumers of his products is, in effect, protection to the farmer, there being a perfect harmony of interest among all the members of the social body.

Less than a year later, Congress redeemed the pledge then given, enacting into law the determination of the many thousands present at the Chicago Convention, a protective tariff having received the assent of Mr. Buchanan on the day before his quitting office. By it full protection was secured to the cotton manufacturer, and this was *then* most gladly accepted by the men of Massachusetts, the Cotton States having left the Union, and the danger of "stimulating domestic competition" having altogether ceased.

For means to carry on the war an internal revenue, however, came soon after to be required, and, as usual, the mining interest was made to suffer; taxes being piled upon iron at its every stage from the pig to the engine, while duties on the most important of all its products, railroad bars, were subsequently so diminished that the difference between contributions by the domestic and foreign article fell to little more than that which resulted from the fact that gold was required for the latter, while greenbacks sufficed for the former.

So long as the war endured, and the premium on gold continued large, this latter furnished all the protection which seemed to be required. With the peace, however, this so far died away as to produce a necessity for such change in the tariff as would tend to counteract the nullification of protection caused by demand, for public use, for contributions on almost every article at every stage of manufacture. To this end the Secretary of the Treasury appointed a Commission, upon whose report was based a tariff bill which finally passed the House in the second week of July, 1866, and was on the following day received in the Senate. A senator from Iowa forthwith moved that its consideration be postponed until the following December; and in the debate on this motion you yourself, as representative of the manufacturing interests of your State, spoke as follows :—

"I shall vote, Mr. President, to commit this bill to the Committee on Finance, with instructions to report early in December. I shall so vote because I believe the permanent interests of the whole country demand that the adjustment of the tariff should be made after the most thorough examination, research, and care. Congress cannot take too much time, nor devote too much attention, to the proper adjustment of a measure that so deeply concerns the revenues of the Government and the varied productive interests of the country. * * *

"What I objected to the other day, and what I object to now, is, that New England should be singled out and charged with the sin of the paternity of this measure. While the representatives of Massachusetts and of New England have voted on general principles for this bill, they have so voted with a great deal of hesitation, doubt, and reluctance. They saw what was clear to the comprehension of gentlemen of ordinary intelligence, that this measure imposed increased duties upon raw material, increased largely the cost of production, and subjected the manufacturing and mechanical interests of their section to the censure and hostility of those who spare no occasion to manifest their hostility to that section of our country."

Here, as ever, "cheap raw material" is, as you see, the one object to be accomplished. Pending the existence of the reciprocity treaty Nova Scotia coal had come in free of duty, and Boston capitalists had, as it is understood, become largely interested in the properties by which it had been supplied. The treaty having been abrogated, the special protection they had so long enjoyed was now to cease, and the fact that this new tariff bill did not provide for continued import of coal duty free, constituted the main objection to it. Here, as everywhere, the mining interests were made the object of attack; "cheap raw materials," whether "lead or tin, brass or iron," being, as you had told the Senate in 1857, essential to your constituents. Who, however, would, in this case of coal, have paid the duty? The manufacturers? Not one cent of it. The man who *must* go to market *must pay the cost of getting there*, as is so well known to the farmer of Iowa who sells for a few cents a bushel of corn that in Massachusetts would command almost a dollar. The price of coal is fixed by the domestic supply, and to that the importer must conform, whatever may be the cost of transportation, or charges of the revenue. The Boston owners of coal mines would have been required to pay the duty fixed by the bill before the Senate, yet was no effort spared for inducing the people of Massachusetts, and of New England generally, to believe that it was a tax to be paid by *them*.

In the division that ensued we find extremists of the North and South combined for destruction of the common enemy, the miner and the laborer—Massachusetts and Kentucky voting together for postponing a measure having for its object the "stimulation of domestic competition" for purchase of the rude products of mining and agricultural labor; and New York and Massachusetts giving all the votes required for securing postponement of this important bill to another session.

At the next session a bill, nearly similar, passed the Senate; and now we find in the House a near approach to the senatorial action of the previous year. The majority of the latter was decidedly favorable to protection, and the state of the country demanded that it should be given. By no direct action could the bill be defeated; but here, as everywhere, there were indirect modes of accomplishing that which directly could not be done. Its management fell into the hands of a representative of Boston capitalists, and the result exhibits itself in the prostration of the industrial interests of the country; and in the fact, that not only do we export all the gold received from California, but that we are running in debt to Europe to an annual amount little less than $200,000,000. In this way it is that we are carrying into practical effect "the democratic idea of the Declaration of Independence," making our people from day to day more dependent on the capitalists of Massachusetts and of Europe.

It may be asked, however, if the Boston capitalist engaged in the cotton manufacture does not suffer equally with those elsewhere engaged in other industrial departments? He does not. Having secured an almost entire monopoly, all he desires is that nothing shall be done that will "stimulate domestic competition;" and to that end, as I understand, New England men have shown themselves inflexibly opposed to the granting of any more protection than that which they themselves required, or little more than that now allowed them. With them capital abounds, interest is low, and machinery exists in great perfection. Just now, they suffer in some small degree; but they find their compensation in the fact that, as before in 1848, and again in 1857, their competitors in the purchase of cotton and sale of cloth, are being ruined beyond redemption. In this State nearly all the mills have been already stopped, and the effect of this well exhibits itself in the fact that Eastern journalists now tell us, that "factory cloths are easy, with an upward tendency in prices, the stocks in first hand in all New England not exceeding 150,000 pieces." The more frequent the crises, the more dangerous the trade; and the more the free-trade cry can be raised, as is now being done throughout New England, the less is the danger of "domestic competition" for the purchase of cotton and for the sale of cotton cloth; and therefore is it that Eastern cotton manufacturers have been enabled to build up the immense fortunes that we find recorded. The system here pursued by them closely resembles that of the great British iron-masters, as below described; the latter being as much intent upon having a monopoly of the supply of iron to the world as are the capitalists of Boston upon monopolizing that of cottons for the Union.

" The laboring classes generally, in the manufacturing districts of this country, and especially in the iron and coal districts, are very little aware of the extent to which they are often indebted for their being employed at all to the immense *losses* which their employers voluntarily incur in bad times, in order *to destroy foreign competition, and to gain and keep possession of foreign markets.* Authentic instances are well known of employers having in such times carried on their works at a loss amounting in the aggregate to three or four hundred thousand pounds in the course of three or four years. If the efforts of those who encourage the combinations to restrict the amount of labor and to produce strikes were to be successful for any length of time, the great accumulations of capital could no longer be made *which enable a few of the most wealthy capitalists to overwhelm all foreign competition in times of great depression,* and thus to clear the way for the *whole trade* to step in when prices revive, and to carry on a great business before *foreign* capital can again accumulate to such an extent as to be able to establish a competition in prices with any chance of success. *The large capitals of this country are the great instruments of warfare against the competing capitals of foreign countries,* and are *the most essential* instruments now remaining by which our manufacturing supremacy can be maintained; the other elements—cheap labor, abundance of raw materials, means of communication, and skilled labor—being rapidly in process of being equalized."

For "iron and coal" read cotton, and for "foreign competition" read "domestic competition," and you will have an almost perfect history of Massachusetts policy for the last twenty years.

Such, as I understand it, is the true history of your State in relation to the question of *real* freedom of trade, *real* freedom for the men who labor, *real* love for the whole Union, and *real* tendency towards enabling freedmen of the South in any manner to profit by the "bloody struggles" through which they and we have so lately passed; and which you here describe as the "struggle on this continent between the democratic idea of the Declaration of Independence and human bondage." The one great object to be accomplished has been that of having "cheap raw materials" at whatsoever cost to the miner and laborer, black or white; and to that end there has been coalition with Canada and Carolina against the West; with Nova Scotia and the South against the Centre; with any and everybody, indeed, that could be made to contribute towards placing the State you represent in the same position as regarded the Union as is now occupied by Britain in reference to the world at large. If it has, in any of its parts, been misrepresented, I shall be most glad to give publicity to any correction that may seem to be required. Postponing, for the present, all remarks thereon, I shall, in another letter, present for your consideration a similar review of the action of this State as representative of the mining interests, of all others the most important in, and to, the Union: meantime remaining,

Yours, faithfully,

HENRY C. CAREY.

Hon. Henry Wilson.

Philadelphia, Sept., 1867.

LETTER SIXTH.

Dear Sir:—

The cotton manufacturer, at a time of serious crisis, discharges some of his hands, putting the rest on half or quarter time and holding himself ready, on the instant when danger shall have ceased, to go ahead and reimburse himself for all that he had lost; doing this by means of higher prices consequent upon the suppression of "domestic competition" that had been brought about.

With those engaged in supplying fuel all is widely different. Mines must be kept free from water whether coal is shipped or not, and pumping is an expensive process. Timbers decay, iron rusts, and both need to be replaced. Coal that should be mined, but for which no market can be found, now falls, and tracks become encumbered—the general result being, as I have always understood, that the difference to the operator from maintaining a mine in idleness on one hand, or full work at the other, is so small as scarcely to be imagined by those not familiar with mining operations. Stoppage to him, therefore, is almost utter ruin. To go ahead is little worse, and therefore is it that the mining record of the State furnishes an exhibition so appalling of the ruin of active, intelligent men to whose energetic action the country has stood indebted for the cheap fuel now in daily use; that fuel to which your State, as well as all New England, owes the development of its manufacturing industry; and that by means of which, alone, we have so recently been enabled to maintain the great blockade, and to pass successfully through the war.

The mine and the furnace, bases of the industrial pyramid, are always the first that are, by reason of absence of demand for their products, compelled to stop. They are, too, always and necessarily last to resume operations. The tariff of 1842 was, so far as the value of coal property had been concerned, wholly inoperative until the autumn of 1844, at which time the manufacturers of Massachusetts, profiting by that annihilation of "domestic competition" for the purchase of cotton or the sale of cloth which had resulted from repeated British free-trade crises, had more than repaid themselves for all the losses they had suffered. So has it lately been; the first two years of the tariff of 1861 having enabled your people to make enormous fortunes, coal meanwhile remaining almost as stagnant as before. The war was more than half over before the occurrence of any essential change in the value of coal property or the profits of coal shippers. Were we now to have a restoration of the societary circulation, several years would be required for restoring the coal region to anything approaching to life and vigor; Massachusetts meanwhile accumulating hundreds of millions of dollars, and going on her way rejoicing. The need of the miner for regularity of the social movement as much exceeds that of the manufacturer as that of the latter exceeds that of the keeper of a grog-shop.

To a great extent, however, the damage done can never be repaired. Mines having been allowed to fill up, coal has been abandoned. The little that could be readily obtained has been dragged out and sent to market, leaving enormous masses to go to waste. To such an extent has this been the case that it is now safe to say, that for *each* ton that has gone to market, *three* have been utterly wasted. Therefore is it that although the whole quantity shipped in more than forty years scarcely exceeds, if indeed it equals, eighteen months' supply for Britain, a very considerable proportion of the region has been entirely exhausted, and very much of it so scratched over as to have caused damage that can never be repaired. The industrial history of the world may be searched in vain for any so wanton waste of wealth, happiness, and national power, as has, by aid of the combined efforts of British and Eastern free-trade believers in "cheap raw materials," and in the advantages of cheap labor, been perpetrated in the coal region of Pennsylvania.

For all these reasons the mining regions of the country—those regions of which Pennsylvania is the representative—require more than any others, such a policy as tends to make of that Declaration of Independence to which you have referred, something more than a mere form of words—such an one as tends to give steadiness of action to the societary machine. Has Massachusetts policy tended in that direction? Look, I pray you, to the exhibit thereof presented in my last, and satisfy yourself if much of the instability of the last twenty years has, or has not, thence resulted; and if the question might not now be fairly put as to whether, even to-day, the danger to the Centre of close political connection with an almost exclusively trading community like that you represent, looking, as it has always done, exclusively to the cheapening of raw materials at the cost of their producers, is not fully as great as has ever been that of a connection with planting communities like those of Alabama or Mississippi. To my mind it appears to be even greater, and it is my belief that conviction to this effect will, without a total change of Massachusetts policy, at no distant day force itself upon the minds of the people of the central and mining States.

To the Union at large the development of Pennsylvania coal mines has been worth thousands of millions of dollars. To that it has been due that you have found yourself enabled to say in your Address that "we have triumphed;" that "we are proud and strong;" that "we have lifted the country towards the heavens;" that "we are a greater people than ever before." But for Pennsylvania anthracite not one word of this could now be said. The cause of the North would this day be "the lost cause," had the chance of war closed the sources from which the coal has been derived; and yet, so far as relates to the persons who have supplied the means required for its development, *it would have been very far better if not a ton of anthracite had ever been found in the State;* or, if found, it had been left where it had first been placed. Had the whole anthracite region, and the improvements of every kind in and leading to it, on the 1st of January, 1861, been appraised at the price in money it would have then commanded, and to the sum then obtained had there been added all the rents and dividends to that day received, the gross amount would not, in my belief, have even been equal to two-thirds of the money that had been given to the work of development, *leaving wholly out of view any price originally paid for the land itself.* It had enriched all but those who had done the work.

Half a dozen years having since elapsed, it might be well, perhaps, for you to pay a visit to the region, and satisfy yourself as to its present condition and its prospects in the future. Doing this, you would find thousands of men, victims of the "cheap raw material" system, wholly unemployed, and very many whose wives and children stand much in need of increased supplies of food and clothing. Looking to the machine shops to which you had been indebted for power to close the southern ports against blockade-runners, you would find them idle. Inquiring for the mechanics, you would learn that not only had they long been unemployed, but that there existed little prospect of demand for the services they so much desired to render. Passing around among the mines, you would be told that where they had not been utterly abandoned, their maintenance had, for a long time past, been rapidly eating up all the profits on the coal supplied to the various workshops by means of which republican armies had been enabled to achieve the great "triumph" of which you speak. Asking for the remnant of the troops which, on receipt of the first advice of danger, and in advance of the men of Massachusetts, had so promptly rushed to the rescue, you might, as I think, find that their wives and children had become candidates for poor-house quarters. Having carefully studied all these things, you might next, perhaps, inquire what had been the effect of paralysis so perfect upon the owners of all this vast property, valuable as it had been supposed to be. In answer, you might be told, that you had before you, in a single valley, 70,000 acres, richer in coal than any other in the world, nearest of all to market, and best supplied with roads; which yet would give to their unfortunate proprietors little more than would be required for paying the additional war taxes, leaving wholly out of view those required of old for education, maintenance of the roads, and other local purposes. Such, in my belief, is the actual fact.

Taking now a bird's-eye view of the whole region, you might, on full reflection, be led to the conclusion that the vote of last year in favor of the Massachusetts system, that one which looks to the cheapening of raw materials and to the establishment of a single market for the Union, had cost, to it alone, a sum more than, if so applied, would purchase all the cotton and woollen mills of your State, and all the houses of the people that in them were employed.

Let the people of Massachusetts now, for a moment, change places with those of this State, finding themselves and their property so placed, and then reflect what would probably be *their* modes of thought and action. Might they not be led to think that further political connection with us was a thing to be dreaded, and not desired. Might they not be disposed to inquire into the effects that had resulted from an improper accumulation of power in the hands of 3,000,000 at one extremity of the Union? Might they not begin to see that sectionalism at the North was as greatly to be dreaded as sectionalism at the South? Might they not be led to arrive at the conclusion, that the work of reconstruction could not be regarded as having been achieved so long as the whole nation should be required to aid in the construction of an inverted pyramid, the little apex of which was to find its place among the mills of Lowell and of Manchester? Might they not, finally, be brought to a *determination* that what really was needed was not so much *reconstruction* as the *construction* of a true pyramid, with a base so broad as to enable it to cover every part of that great farming and mining region—the richest in the world—which, with exception of that small portion of the mere surface occupied by extremists North and South, is co-extensive with the Union, and embraces all its territories from the Lakes to the Gulf, and from the Atlantic to the Pacific? I think they would. If, then, such would probably be, when so placed, their modes of thought, what *should be now* the modes of thought and action of those who really own the State, and who so long have found themselves, as between the upper and the nether millstone, ground between the rival States of Carolina and Massachusetts?

Leaving you to reflect on the answer proper to be given to this important question, I remain, for the present,

Yours, faithfully,

HENRY C. CAREY.

Hon. Henry Wilson.

Philadelphia, September 10, 1867.

LETTER SEVENTH.

Dear Sir:—

Massachusetts is the type of that portion of our population which has its home north of the 41st parallel, and which, more than any other, finds in trade the chief occupation of life. In like manner, in Pennsylvania is found the type of that which occupies the territory between 39° 30' and 41°, and with which farming and mining, and the conversion of the rude products of both, make most demand for physical and mental force. Of that force, she is, and has always been, the representative, and therefore has it always been, that as she has gone so has gone the Union. What has been her course in the past, and what are her claims in the present for occupation of a position so important, it is proposed now to show.

The Constitution, as completed by the Convention of 1787, gave great satisfaction to the smaller States, placing them, as it did, on an equal senatorial footing with the larger ones, and securing them against that absorption by these latter which had been not a little dreaded. Would, however, Massachusetts be content to accept as an equal in political power the little Rhode Island? Would Virginia be so by Delaware? or Pennsylvania by the little State beyond the Delaware?

First to answer this question was Pennsylvania, the call of a Convention for the purpose of considering the Constitution having been issued almost instantly on learning that the general Convention had completed the work intrusted to its hands. First, with exception of little Delaware, she ratified it, doing this by the large majority of two to one, and thus setting an example of magnanimity which was but very slowly followed. First of the large States to follow was Massachusetts, but her action long remained in doubt, and the majority was but 19 in a body of 355. Some months later came the Virginia Convention, and here the doubt was greater still. Ratification was, however, at length effected by the meagre majority of 10 out of 160. From the first New York had been opposed to union, and the signature of but one of her representatives in the Convention, that of Hamilton, is appended to the Constitution. Very late in taking it into consideration, the opposition in the State Convention proved then so fierce as to make it in the highest degree doubtful if ratification could be at all obtained. When, however, it had been ascertained that nine States, the necessary number, had at length given in their adhesion—that formation of the Union could in no possible manner be prevented—that power had already been given to a Federal government that might be used coercively—then, and not till then, was ratification obtained; and yet, by little more than a bare majority, the ayes having exceeded the noes by only three.

But for the prompt and decided action of Pennsylvania the Union would not have been formed. But for her steady adhesion since it could not have been maintained. By the one she earned the title of the Keystone State; by the other she has, as I propose to show, vindicated her claim thereto.

Five and twenty years later we find in Massachusetts the first attempt at secession, followed a few years after by Carolina nullification of the law, as preparation for further and more decided action. On both occasions Pennsylvania stood unflinchingly by the Union. From that hour the question of its further maintenance rested with her, and *her alone.* Had she been willing to abandon her Northern friends, she might, as is well known, have made her own terms. Offers of every kind were made to her. Always faithful, she treated them with that contempt they merited, and the records of Congress would, as I think, be searched in vain for evidence that she had ever, even for a moment, been willing to profit herself at the cost of any whatsoever of the great national interests. The greatest of all, the maintenance of the Union, was in her especial keeping; and on that head she now stands before the world with a record that is without a parallel in the world.

First at the ballot-box in 1860, she, by the vast majority given to Gov. Curtin, decided the question between Messrs. Lincoln and Breckinridge. First again at the ballot-box in the dark hours of 1863, she saved the Union at a time when both New York and New Jersey had passed under the control of sympathizers with the rebellion. Had she then failed, the Union would have perished.

First in the field in 1861, her hardy miners preceded, by a single day, the men of Massachusetts. First to appreciate the importance of prompt exertion, she raised and equipped an army of sixteen thousand men, of whom not so much as a fifth returned from the field unharmed. Placing at the head of her divisions the best officers of the State, she tendered them to the nation, and had they been as promptly accepted as they had been promptly raised, the result of the Bull Run battle would have been widely different.

First to appreciate the importance of social organization, the loyal men of her commercial capital set the example of forming themselves into a League for controlling and directing the public opinion of the State—and with what effect I need not tell you. Leaving wholly out of view its other important services, it stands now alone as an association of individuals that had, at their own private cost, placed ten full regiments in the field.

First to feel that every private, of whatsoever State, was to be regarded as the people's friend, that city fed, and kindly cared for, every man of the many hundreds of thousands who passed from north to south, or from south to north.

Alone in the possession of anthracite, whose development had caused the ruin of most of those concerned therein, she furnished nearly all the motive power that maintained the blockade; that kept in operation all the mills and shops from which the Union obtained its rifles and its cannon, its cloth and its ships, and most of its internal revenue.

Alone in the possession of furnaces and rolling-mills in quantity sufficient for doing the greatly needed work, their owners, then so recently denounced by Eastern friends as little better than public robbers, supplied nearly all the iron needed by mills and shops throughout the Union.

Without Mr. Lincoln, without Stanton or Grant, without Meade or Sheridan, without any other State, the war might, perhaps, have been brought to a successful conclusion. Without HER no war could have been maintained for even a single hour. Had Lee succeeded at Gettysburg, he would have controlled the sources of national power, and the war would have been ended. Then, as ever, as Pennsylvania went, so has gone the Union. As she may in future go, so *must* the Union go; all the obstacles that have, till now, stood in the way of combined Central and Southern action having been removed.

Having thus shown what had been her course in the recent eventful years, allow me now to ask that you should re-read my last, and satisfy yourself as to what has been her compensation. Look at her abandoned mines! Look at her closed-up rolling and spinning-mills! Then, I pray, re-peruse the adverse speeches that have been made in Congress in reference to her interests; *interests a hundred-fold greater in national importance than some of those in regard to which our Eastern friends have been accustomed to be so eloquent.*

Leaving out of view, however, her own private interests, it is her duty, as GUARDIAN OF THE UNION, to look to those of the whole people, North and South, East and West, and satisfy herself what has thus far been the result of a commercial policy whose tendencies have all been in the direction of giving to the East an entire monopoly of the cotton manufacture, while depriving the most important portions of the Union of all power to avail themselves of the vast mineral wealth in which their territories so much abound. Doing this, as she *must* now do, she meets with the striking facts in regard to cotton cloth, and iron, that will now be given :—

Twenty years since the domestic consumption of cotton had reached 600,000 bales, being the equivalent of . . . . . . pounds 250,000,000
The import of foreign cottons was then about
40,000,000 yards, equal, probably, to pounds 6,000,000

Total, 256,000,000

The population was then about 20,000,000, and this would
3

give a total consumption of more than 12 pounds per head; and a growth, in five years of full and complete protection, of fully 70 per cent.

Last year the domestic consumption required, as I am informed, 700,000 bales. This year it will need but little more than 600,000. Taking it, however, at even 650,000, we obtain, say, . . . pounds 270,000,000
The import of the first four months of the year was 20,000,000 yards; at which rate we should have for the year 60,000,000, the equivalent of probably . . . pounds 10,000,000

Total, 280,000,000

Within this period we have mined of the precious metals to the extent of some twelve or fifteen hundred millions of dollars. Nevertheless, instead of an increase, we have large decrease, the consumption, per head, having fallen *from twelve pounds down to eight;* the quantity being little more than it had been when the pro-slavery tariff of 1846 came into practical operation. Such have been the results of the policy which has looked to the cheapening of raw materials; to the discouragement of "domestic competition" for their purchase; and to the practical subjugation of the miners, farmers, and laborers engaged in their production! The Massachusetts system has in view nothing beyond enrichment of the capitalist, while that of Pennsylvania tends towards giving to labor that real freedom which results from growing competition for its purchase. Of the two, which, my dear sir, has most tended to "destroy human bondage?"

In 1842 our production of iron was about 220,000 tons, and our total consumption, of foreign and domestic, about 300,000. Five years later, the production, as stated by Mr. Walker, and as subsequently confirmed by the iron-masters themselves, was 700,000. The import was then about 100,000, giving a total of 800,000, and an increase, under thorough protection, in the five years that had then elapsed, of 167 per cent.

Twenty years have since passed, throughout a large proportion of which it has pleased the representatives of Massachusetts to array themselves on the side of cotton-planters, slave owners, railroad monopolists, and all other opponents of real freedom, against the people of the mining regions of the country, the result now exhibiting itself in the following facts, to wit: that the average product of the last three years has been but 1,100,000 tons; that the quantity this year made will be less than that of the last by 200,000 tons; that the import of the year will probably reach 200,000, in payment for which we are sending by every steamer all the gold yielded by the Pacific and Mountain States; that the total consumption of the year will, in actual quantity, be but 65 per cent. greater than that of 1847, although our population has almost doubled; that the consumption per head, which had more than doubled in the protective years from 1842 to 1847, has now fallen to less than it then had been; and that, as the consumption of iron furnishes the best of all tests of advancing civilization, we must have gone forward rapidly under protection, and have been retro-grading ever since its abandonment in 1847.

In facts like those here presented, in relation to both cotton and iron, there is found, as it seems to me, no evidence that we are likely long to have to boast "that we are a greater people than ever before;" or that "hereafter, in the future, we shall be friends and brothers as we were in the morning of the Republic." Had the tariff of 1842 been maintained, we should be now making of the one 4,000,000 tons a year, and consuming or ex-porting in the shape of cloth, 3,000,000 bales of the other; the nation becoming *really* great, the colored population of the South, meanwhile, peacefully advancing with profit to themselves and their owners towards a freedom far more perfect than that which, at the cost of hundreds of thousands of lives, and thousands of millions of property, they have as yet obtained.

To all this, however, in the eyes of the capitalists of New and Old England, there would have been one objection, to wit, that it would have greatly raised the prices of raw materials throughout the South—land, labor, and the rude products of both. It would have made a market on the land for both food and cotton, and would so have facilitated consumption of the latter that the price would never have been below $80 per bale. It would have made throughout the South that compe-tition for purchase of human force, physical and mental, which would have "destroyed human bondage." It would have made throughout the Centre and the South a network of roads that would have tied together all the States of the Union just as now are bound together those of the little and compact New England. Giving us, quietly and profitably to all, an universal freedom, we should have gone gently ahead towards the *construction* of a "more perfect Union," and would have been spared the present necessity for *reconstruction.*

You speak of the "warm and generous greetings" with which the South will now be welcomed. What is there needed is, how-ever, something more than a mere form of words. The ballot-box is of little use for filling the stomach, or for repairing roads. The South sees the price of cotton steadily falling, until it has now, in Liverpool, reached ten-pence, the equivalent of twenty-eight cents. Why is this? Because, under the industrial and finan-cial policy now advocated by Massachusetts, the domestic con-sumption, instead of rising this year, as it should have done, to 1,100,000 bales, has fallen to 650,000, at a cost to the South, on a crop of 2,500,000 bales, of $100,000,000.

Such, my dear sir, are the "greetings" thus far given by Massachusetts to Carolina, Georgia, and Alabama. Let those

of the future be of the same character, and the day will not
then be far distant when you and your fellow-citizens will find
yourselves compelled to the conclusion that you had been quite
in error when you had said that "all our troubles had passed
away forever." British free-trade built up slavery and made the
rebellion. Let it be maintained, and it will defeat all your efforts
at reconstruction.

Yours, very truly,
HENRY C. CAREY.

Hon. Henry Wilson.

Philadelphia, Sept., 1867.

LETTER EIGHTH.

Dear Sir :—

The *greatness* of our country, of which, in common with so
many of its people, you so recently have spoken, is, as you see,
being manifested not only by a diminished power over our own
mineral deposits, but by a diminution in the ratio of consumption,
whether of domestic or foreign production, to population. Why
is it that such has been, and now is, the case? Is it because of
any deficiency in the quantity of ores at our command? That
you may yourself answer this question, I here, leaving this State
wholly out of consideration, present you with an account, by a
recent traveller, of some of the midland counties of Virginia, as
follows :—

"I have rambled over the best portions of Goochland, Fluvianna, and
Buckingham Counties, mixed freely with their people in all conditions of
life, and witnessed an amount of mineral wealth of which you in the
North have not the remotest conception—an amount of wealth quite equal
to, if not in some instances surpassing anything to be found in California.
I know that much of what I am about to tell you may be received with
incredulity; but facts are stubborn things, and nothing is easier than for
those who may doubt me to come here and look with their own eyes.

"That Virginia contains the precious metals every geologist and
mineralogist has long been aware; and there can be but few intelligent
readers who are ignorant of the fact that enormous fortunes have been
extracted from isolated places of wide reputation—such, for instance, as
the London Mine, in Buckingham County, in this State. But very few, I
venture to say, know the vast amount of treasure which runs through Virginia in her entire length—a distance of not less than two hundred miles,
by at least sixty miles in width.

"In that magnificent belt of richness, revealed to her by the same
mighty convulsion which heaved the Blue Ridge chain of mountains
from her womb, are to be found, in the greatest abundance, gold, silver,
copper, iron, platinum, cinnabar, lead, plumbago, tin, coal, roofing-slate of
the most durable kind, marble of the rarest beauty and perfection, and a
variety of other valuable mineral substances—such as gypsum, limestone
soapstone, hone-stone, equal to anything Turkey ever produced—too long
for enumeration."

What is here said of these few counties is almost equally true in reference to the whole uplands of the South, fuel and ores, and especially iron ore, abounding to an extent wholly unknown in any other country of the world; and it is in behalf of that region of marvellous mineral and metallic wealth, as well as in her own, that Pennsylvania has asked protection. The idea of preventing the growth of "domestic competition" for the purchase of ores, or for the sale of iron, finds, as I am happy to say, no place in *her* record.

Among the richest of the States in these respects is Alabama, fuel abounding and her ores being fitted, as I understand, for production of iron fully equal in quality to the very best obtained in Pennsylvania.

Crossing the Mississippi, we find in North Louisiana, according to a report recently made to the Legislature by the Hon. Mr. Robertson,

"Iron ore so abundant as absolutely, at some points, to obstruct agriculture. Vast heaps of rich ores may be seen piled up in the fields. In De Soto and West Nachitoches is a vast field of granular and argillaceous ores, many miles in extent. This iron field lies north and northeast of Pleasant Hill, and all the necessary concomitants for the successful manufacture of iron are to be found in convenient proximity and in great abundance. A large portion of Claiborne and Bienville is an immense iron bed. Jackson and Winn are also rich in their beds of iron ore. The superficial surface ores, brown hematite and granular, of these parishes, would supply hundreds of furnaces for years to come. Seven miles east of Minden is a rich field of iron, lying for miles around the base of Fort Hill, a huge hill which rises above the surrounding country in three distinct and broad terraces. Around the outer edges of these terraces are natural embankments of arenaceous boulders, each embankment some seven or eight feet in height. This bed of ore extends to within four miles of Minden on the northeast, and from that point it may be continuously traced through Mount Lebanon, and nearly to Sparta, in Bienville parish. The region around Mount Lebanon is peculiarly rich in valuable ores."

From the iron mountain of Missouri to the near neighborhood of the Gulf such ores abound, and in a profusion of which the European world has no conception, yet is our consumption, per head, less than it had been when Congress, under the lead of Mr. Walker, abandoned the road towards freedom for all, black and white, to re-enter upon that pro-slavery one to which we had been indebted for the numerous crises which had occurred between 1837 and 1842.

These are striking facts, and such as would, in any other country, command the consideration of men professing to be statesmen. Here, however, they are not regarded as sufficient to offset the demand for cheap iron made by Massachusetts makers of pins or penknives who fail to see that the greater the "domestic competition" for the sale of their raw material, the cheaper must it become, and the greater the growth of the domestic commerce the more must be the demand for both pins and knives.

Turning now to France, badly supplied with ores, and compelled to look for coal to Belgium and to Britain, we find the domestic production and total consumption, foreign and domestic, in the last six years, to have grown as follows :—

	Production.		Consumption.	
	Pig—tons	Iron—tons.	Tons.	Tons.
1860 . . .	880.000	560,000	935,000	500,000
1861 . . .	890,000	672,000	1,030,000	550,000
1862 . . .	1,070,000	700,000	1,270,000	788,000
1863 . . .	1,150,000	790,000	1,330,000	790,000
1864 . . .	1,175,000	795,000	1,270,000	735,090
1865 . . .	1,191,000	848,000	1,320,000	810,000

With no perceptible increase of population, the average increase of these quantities is about 50 per cent. In twenty years of British free-trade, and its attendant crises, our own has retrograded in its ratio to numbers, when it should have quite quadrupled. Seeing all this, I find myself unable to see how we can fairly make the boast, that " we are greater than we ever were before."

It may be said, however, that is the free-trade period, and so it *will* be said by those who find their profit in blinding our people's eyes to the fact that French free-trade meant merely the passage from prohibition to highly protective duties ; and, that the protection this day enjoyed by those engaged in developing the mineral resources of France, is fully equal to that given by our tariff of 1861, before internal taxes had so nearly nullified the little that had been granted. In proof of this permit me to refer you to the following comparative table :—

Names of Articles.	Quantities.	French duties under the Reciprocity treaty in American money.	U. S. duties under the Morrill tariff.
Iron, pig, and old cast iron .	ton.	$4 39	$6 00
Iron, old broken wrought . .	ton.	6 35	6 00
Iron, bar	ton.	13 68	15 00
Iron, railroad	ton.	13 68	12 00
Iron, sheet	ton.	25 41 to $31 28	20 to $25
Iron manufactures ; pipes and solid columns . . .	ton.	8 30	11 20
Iron manufac. ; heavy wrought	ton.	17 58	20 00
Iron manufactures ; small wares	ton.	29 39	22 40
Iron manufactures ; cut nails .	cwt.	97¾	1 12
Iron manufactures ; wr't nails	cwt.	1 46½	2 24
Iron manufactures ; anchors, chains, cables . . .	ton.	19 54	30 to $33
Iron manufactures ; tubes of wrought iron, large . .	ton.	25 40	44 80
Iron manufactures ; tubes of wrought iron, small . .	ton.	48 85	44 80
Steel in bars of all kinds . .	lb.	1 3-10c.	1¼ and 2c.
Steel in sheets above 1-12th of an inch thick . . .	lb.	2c.	2c. and 15 ℔c.
Steel in sheets under 1-12th of an inch thick . . .	lb.	2¼c.	2¼ and 15 ℔c.
Steel tools in pure steel . .	lb.	3¼c.	30 ℔ cent.
Steel sewing needles . .	lb.	8¼ to 17½c.	20 ℔ cent.

Of far more importance, however, than any moderate difference in the amount of duty, is the fact that in France development of the mineral resources of the country is held to be a matter of national importance. *Canaille* like those, jew and gentile, gratuitously supplied by England for teaching our legislators how to obtain cheap iron, are there not tolerated, Frenchmen having too much self-respect to permit such interference in their domestic arrangements. The iron man of France can, therefore, go confidently ahead, making the large investments required for facilitating cheap production. Here, on the contrary, *as if with a determination that iron never shall be cheap,* the sword of Damocles is always held suspended over him, and he perishes at last for the simple reason that no one dares to lend him the amount required for making the improvements that are needed. Had our legislation in the past exhibited anything like common sense, or real national feeling, we should have now no need for measures of reconstruction.

How rapid has been, and now is, the German progress will be seen on an examination of the following facts: In 1850, the product of steel was valued at $350,000. Ten years later it had reached $1,400,000. Five years still later, having meantime endowed the world with the great gift of the Bessemer process, the figure reached was $10,000,000. In 1850, the total value of pig and wrought iron was but $15,000,000; whereas, in 1865, it had grown to $55,000,000; and all this vast increase was but preparation for new and further movements in the same direction, arrangements, as we are told, having recently been made for great extension of operations.

Five and thirty years of protection have sufficed for constructing the greatest empire of Europe—a true pyramid, based upon the mineral and metallic resources of the State. The same five and thirty years have been by us expended in the effort to create an inverted pyramid with its apex resting upon the cotton and woollen mills of Massachusetts; and with such success that, after expending thousands of millions of dollars, wasting property to the amount of other thousands of millions, and destroying lives to the extent of hundreds of thousands, we are now engaged in an effort at *reconstructing* the rickety edifice, taking no note of the fact that its permanent existence would be in opposition to all experience, as it would be certainly opposed to all the teachings of science.

Were it this day possible so to raise the duties on iron, and commodities of which iron is the chief component, as to make them almost prohibitive, at the same time giving assurance that, despite the claims of pin or penknife-makers, the protection so granted should endure for even one decade; were it possible, I say, to do this, the close of that period would see iron cheaper here than elsewhere in the world; we should then export iron instead of gold ; and then it might be possible to speak with truth of our existing *greatness.*

Three and thirty years since, when the protective tariff of 1828 had enabled us to extinguish the whole national debt, even that which bore an interest only of three per cent. ; when the treasury was full to overflowing ; when, for the first time, we had achieved a real independence ; when immigration was for the first time growing rapidly ; then, and then only, could we honestly have made any claim to greatness. Seven years later the country was so utterly without credit that the same bankers who had been paid, at par, a loan at three per cent., utterly refused to lend a single dollar at six per cent. Where was *then* our free-trade *greatness?*

Five years later, the tariff of 1842 having meantime *reconstructed* the country, we had become strong enough to dictate law in the halls of the Montezumas, and to add California to the Union. Then, for the second time, might there have been made some little claim to the idea of greatness. Little more, however, than a dozen years of British free-trade next sufficed for rending the Union asunder and placing both the parts at the feet of Britain.

Two years since, when protection and the greenback at home, and British hostility abroad, had combined for promoting material and moral independence, and had enabled us to pass safely through the war, we might again have laid some claim to be considered "great."

Where, however, are we now ? We have a *bigger* country, having added Walrussia to our territories. We have a larger foreign debt than any country of the world. We pay a higher rate of interest than any other with claim to be considered civilized. We produce more of the precious metals than any other, and so perfect is our independence that not a dollar of either gold or silver can be retained. We have the *friendship* of England, and it clings to us as pertinaciously and destructively as did the poisoned shirt of Nessus to the shoulders of Hercules. Having closed our rolling-mills, we now import iron at the monthly rate of $2,000,000, and pay for it in gold-bearing bonds. Having closed our glass-houses, we now import whole cargoes of coal and sand in the shape of window-glass, and pay for them in the gold of California. Having destroyed the demand for coal, we are now destroying the powers of the land itself by which that coal is yielded. Having reduced the consumption of cotton to little beyond the point at which it had stood twenty years since, and having thus compelled so large an export as to have already reduced the British price to ten-pence, we have imposed a tax upon our reconstructed brethren of the South, of probably $100,000,000, and this at a time when they specially need our aid.

Such are the evidences, as they present themselves to my mind, of the *declining greatness* achieved since the peace. Believing that before the close of another decade, if the Massachusetts policy be maintained, you will see the country arrive at a condition even worse than that of 1861, at that perfection of littleness which, forty years since, was exhibited by what is now the *really* great and powerful Germanic empire, I remain, with much regard,*

Yours, very truly,

HENRY C. CAREY

Hon. Henry Wilson.

Philadelphia, Sept., 1867

LETTER NINTH.

Dear Sir:—

Half a century since the vast country west and north of the Ohio, with its extraordinary wealth of soil, that soil, too, underlaid to an extent elsewhere unknown with coal and ores, contained but half a million of inhabitants. From that time to the present its population has gone on increasing until it numbers now a dozen millions; yet, during nearly all that time has it been required by the allied Southern and Eastern States, that its farmers should altogether fail to profit of the great mineral treasures by which they had been everywhere surrounded, and by aid of which they would long since have been enabled to create a great domestic industry and a varied agriculture. The one desired that food might be low in price that they might cheaply feed their negroes; the other desired "cheap raw material" of every kind, that they might obtain and maintain a monopoly of the cotton manufacture. Compelled thus to go abroad for iron, all the materials of which lay beneath their own proper land; compelled, too, to send their wool abroad to be returned in the form of cloth—the people of that vast territory have found themselves limited in their cultivation to those white crops of which the earth yields but little, and which, for that

* Since writing the above I have received a very interesting account of the mining operations of Belgium, giving the following facts:—

From 1850 to 1863 the increase of production was as follows—

Of coal, per cent.	100
" mineral, per cent.	100
" forges and mills, per cent.	300
" foundries, "	250

In proportion to the numbers of her people Belgium now produces eight times as much coal as France, between twice and three times as much as Prussia, only one-fourth less than Great Britain, and the quantity doubles every fifteen years. This, too, occurs in a country whose coal fields scarcely exceed in their extent those of our anthracite region alone, and whose population increases so very slowly that a century and a half would be required for its duplication.

reason, could alone bear carriage to distant markets. Green crops, of which the earth yields by tons instead of bushels, and by means of which the soil is best prepared for white ones, have, as a rule, been interdicted, the cost of transportation to distant cities having been greater than the prices that could be obtained when those cities had been reached. The place of consumption being far distant from that of production no manure could be returned upon the land; and, as a necessary consequence of this, it became yearly poorer than before. The greater its poverty the more imperious became the necessity for change of place, and thus it has been that a few millions of people have been scattered over a surface capable of feeding half the population of the earth. The more they scattered the more did they become subjected to damage to their crops resulting from winters of so intense a cold as to compel them to postpone to spring the sowing of their various seeds. The more they scattered over the prairies the greater became their need for fencing, and for their own protection against the winter's blast, and the greater became the difficulty of bringing from a distance the lumber so much required. The more they scattered the more were they compelled to place their dependence on a single crop, and the greater their losses resulting from excess of moisture or of heat. The more they scattered the greater became the need of roads, and the greater the difficulty of obtaining iron, the ores of which, and the fuel with which to smelt them, lay beneath their feet; they themselves, meanwhile, wasting annually a larger amount of force, physical and mental, than would have been required for erecting furnaces, forges, and rolling mills, in quantity sufficient to supply with iron all the people who could then, or now, be found between the Rocky Mountains and the Atlantic.

The single form that agricultural improvement has taken throughout almost the whole territory has been that of machinery for facilitating the reaping of the crops, large or small, that have been yielded by land from which the soil has been, and is being, annually carried off to distant markets. With every such *improvement* less and less has been consumed at home, the result exhibiting itself in the fact, that the average yield of wheat by the originally fertile soil of Ohio, Indiana, and Illinois, scarcely exceeds, if indeed it equals, a dozen bushels to the acre.

Twenty years since Britain offered to the world, as consideration for abandoning all further efforts at industrial independence, a repeal of her Corn Laws, thereby granting to them the great boon of supplying her few and impoverished artisans with food. Germany, nevertheless, went straight ahead, and so did France, developing their mineral resources, and thus making a market on the land for all its products, the result exhibiting itself in the fact that not only has their consumption of iron increased twice, if not even thrice, more rapidly than the numbers of their respective populations, but that they have fairly distanced Britain in the importance of their inventions, the beauty and the excellence of their iron fabrics. With us the course of things was different; we having promptly swallowed the bait that had so skilfully been proffered. Abandoning the policy of freedom under which our domestic consumption of cotton and our domestic production of iron had, in the short space of four years, almost trebled, we returned to the pro-slavery British free-trade system, the result exhibiting itself in the facts that not only do we now consume less iron per head than we did twenty years since, but that our consumption of cotton is scarcely more in quantity than it then had been.

During nearly the whole of this long period Massachusetts has cried aloud for cheap raw materials, whether corn or cotton, coal, tin, lead, or iron, and to the end that they might be "cheap" she has coalesced with British iron-masters in waging systematic war upon the greatest of all national interests, coal and iron. The result, so far as regards the first, exhibits itself in the fact that, with beds of fuel so vast and rich as to be without a parallel in the world, the quantity this year mined will scarcely exceed, if, indeed, it equals, the *addition* made to the British quantity as compared with that of seven years since.

Such having been the price paid for the privilege of underworking the British agriculturist and supplying the British artisan with "cheap" American food, we may now, for a moment, look to see to what extent the end in view has been obtained.

At the date of the repeal of the Corn Laws the import of wheat into Great Britain, as given in an article just now published, was 1,141,967 quarters, or, in round numbers,

about	.	.	.	.	.	bushels	10,000,000
By 1850 it had grown to		.	.	.	.		44,000,000
In 1858 it was	.	.	.	.	.	.	43,000,000
" 1860 "	.	.	.	.	.	.	59,000,000
" 1861 "	.	.	.	.	.	.	70,000,000
" 1862 "	.	.	.	.	.	.	93,000,000
" 1865 "	.	.	.	.	.	.	48,000,000
" 1866 "	.	.	.	.	.	.	60,000,000

Of these enormous quantities how much have we, owners of what we had been accustomed to look upon as the granary, *par excellence*, of the world, on an average of the last ten years, supplied? Just *sixteen millions*, that being the mess of pottage for which Mr. Secretary Walker sold our birthright, and that being the great trade in whose behalf our Massachusetts friends require that we close our mines and furnaces, and import, duty free, our railroad bars! For every dollar's worth of food that we send to Britain, France sends, as I think, three or four. Why? Because France avails herself of her mineral resources, few and poor as they are, and thus creates a real agriculture! Because, refusing to profit of the almost inconceivably vast mineral wealth at our command, we compel our farmers to export their soil to distant markets, with daily diminution in the power of the land to yield return to labor! Because French policy tends to "stimulate domestic competition" for purchase of the rude products of the field, and for the sale of finished commodities! Because, with us, the extreme North and the extreme South have always been united in a policy whose object has been that of compelling the West to look South or East, and not homeward, for any market for its products. Because the pin and pen-knife makers of the East can command the votes of Massachusetts, at the cost of those who mine the coal and produce the iron by means of which blockades have been maintained.

The "cheap raw material policy" having now, with slight exception, prevailed for twenty years, let us for a moment inquire into the progress thus far made.

In the first four months of the present year the total of our domestic exports was, in round numbers, $184,000,000, the equivalent of $120,000,000 in gold.

Of this Cotton furnished	$108,000,000
Gold	19,000,000
Coal-oil and oil-cake	6,000,000
Tobacco	6,000,000
Breadstuffs and provisions	22,000,000
Lumber, rosin, and turpentine . . .	6,000,000
Whale-oil	1,000,000
Making a total of	$168,000,000,

the products of little else than the rudest labor, and leaving but $16,000,000, the equivalent of $11,000,000 in gold, as the representative of an amount of industrial capacity that has no equal in the world, and that ere this, under a system tending to "stimulate domestic competition," would have placed us in a position to convert the whole of this food and cotton into cloth; to give to the world $50,000,000 per month of commodities whose production would be tending daily towards stimulating into full activity all these faculties for whose development we maintain our public schools.

Men and nations, my dear sir, become greater as they more and more acquire the power of self-direction. France finishes all her commodities, and can go with them *where she will.* We, more enlightened as we think ourselves to be, send forward all our products in their rudest form, and go with them *where we must.* The one requires the world to come to her, and *determines the price they must pay:* the other, always seeking buyers, piles up her goods in Liverpool and Havre, and leaves to French and English manufacturers the power to determine *at what prices they will consent to take them.*

In all this you may see proof that "we are really greater than we ever were before." If growing dependence on the will of foreign traders can be taken as evidence of growing greatness, then are you wholly in the right. If growing independence is to be taken as such evidence, then are the Germans in the right, and the policy they pursue is precisely the antipodes of that now advocated by the literary and political representatives of Massachusetts.

Yours, truly,

HENRY C. CAREY.

Hon. Henry Wilson.

Philadelphia, April, 1867.

LETTER TENTH:

Dear Sir:—

Even before the war a great change had already commenced in regard to the sources from which the northern supplies of cereals were to come, Tennessee and North Carolina furnishing large supplies of wheat greatly superior in quality to that grown on northern lands, and commanding higher prices in all our markets. From further south, and almost to the Gulf, we now learn from an important public document before referred to, that—

"Wherever the United States cavalry camped in Louisiana, during the war, wheat, rye, oats, and barley sprouted from the seed scattered where they fed their horses, and, when undisturbed, headed finely and ripened well—*the extraordinary size and weight of the wheat and barley heads showing that the soil was peculiarly adapted to their growth.* A gentleman, residing in the swamps of Assumption, assures me," says its author, "*that he has raised wheat and rye for twenty-two years, and that he has never had a failure; both grains frequently made forty bushels to the acre.* I have cited these instances to show that wheat has been raised, time and again, under all sorts of circumstances, and on every kind of soil in Louisiana."

In other cases as many as 60 bushels to the acre have been obtained. It ripens in May, and its market value may be judged from the facts that while—

"The daily quotations show that Southern flour, raised in Missouri, Tennessee, and Virginia, brings from three to five dollars more per barrel than the best New York Genesee flour; that of Louisiana and Texas is far superior to the former even, owing to the superior dryness, and the fact that it contains more gluten, and does not ferment so easily. Southern flour makes better dough and maccaroni than Northern or Western flour; it is better adapted for transportation over the sea, and keeps better in the tropics. It is therefore the flour that is sought after for Brazil, Central America, Mexico, and the West India markets, which are at our doors. A barrel of strictly Southern flour will make twenty pounds more bread than Illinois flour, because, being so much dryer, it takes up more water in making up. In addition to this vast superiority of our grain, we have other advantages over the Western States in grain growing. Our climate advances the crop so rapidly that we can cut out our wheat six weeks before a scythe is put into the fields of Illinois; and being so near the Gulf, we avoid the delays in shipping and the long transportation, the cost of which consumes nearly one-half of the product of the West. These advantages, the superior quality of the flour, the earlier harvest, and the cheap and easy shipment, enable us absolutely to forestall the West in the foreign demand, which is now about 40,000,000 of bushels annually, and is rapidly increasing, and also in the Atlantic seaboard trade. Massachusetts, it is calculated, raises not more than one months' supply of flour for her vast population. New York not six month's supply for her population, and the other Atlantic States in like proportion. This vast deficit is now supplied by the Western States, and the trade has enriched the West, and has built railroads in every direction to carry towards the East the gold-producing grain. We can, if we choose, have a monopoly of this immense trade, and the time may not be far distant when, in the dispensation of Providence, the West, *which contributed so largely to the uprooting of our servile system and the destruction of our property, will find that she has forced us into a rivalry against which she cannot compete, and that she will have to draw not only her supplies of cotton, sugar, and rice, but even her breadstuffs from the South.*"

Is it, however, for breadstuffs alone that the North is likely, with our present exhaustive cultivation, to be compelled to look to the South? It is not; the sweet potatoe, which can be grown on "every acre in Louisiana," and of which the yield, even at present, "averages 200 bushels to the acre," having, during the war, been fully tested in feeding hogs, and having, quantity and quality of the pork considered, been found, *pound for pound,* fully equal to Indian corn, of which the average yield of the States north and west of the Ohio is less than a third as much. With careful cultivation it has been known to yield more than 600 bushels, or six times as much as can, with equal care and close to Eastern markets, be obtained of the great staple of the North, thereby enabling those who are in the future to cultivate those rich Southern lands wholly to supersede the Northwest in the work of supplying animal as well as vegetable food to the people of the tropics and of Europe.

Sixty acres to the hand, it is said, may be cultivated in grain. Combining with this the raising of cotton the effect of diversification of agricultural pursuits is thus exhibited:—

"With one-fifth of our former labor, it is, therefore, clearly practicable to put every inch of cleared land under cultivation. Thus, under the present system of labor, a cotton or sugar plantation of 600 acres would require 100 hands to cultivate it exclusively in either cane or cotton, for two years' experience has taught us that five acres to the hand is all that can be successfully accomplished in these crops, while twelve or fifteen active hands will suffice to cultivate and take off fifty acres of cotton and 450 of wheat, rye, or barley, by the aid of the well-tried, improved implements in every-day use at the North and West, and at much less expense for teams than would be required if cotton alone were planted."

Turning now to fruits, we find the State under consideration, which is, however, to a great extent the type of the whole of those bordering on the Gulf, to be capable of yielding "in unusual proportion nearly all those of the other States," and very many of the tropical ones.

"Oranges, superior to those of the West Indies, are grown in all the lower portion of the State, and are rarely hurt by the frost. The trees attain, in some places, a great size. I measured one at Lake Charles, in Calcasieu, eleven years old, which was over thirty feet in height, and, at a foot above the ground, was three feet five and a half inches in circumference, and which, I learned, had produced near 2,500 oranges the past season, one of which weighed eighteen ounces. Bananas have been largely cultivated during the last ten years, and now adorn every dwelling. Citrons, mespilas, lemons, jujubes, pomegranates, guavas, and even pine apples, are cultivated in all Lower Louisiana, while the fig, the pear, the apple, the peach, the plum, the apricot, the nectarine, the quince, the cherry, the almond, and every variety of grape and currant, grow in every part of the State. Dewberries, blackberries, mulberries, gooseberries, huckle or whortleberries, strawberries, and raspberries, are found as wild and indigenous fruits. The peaches, pears, and figs of Louisiana are peculiarly sweet and luscious. Fruit-raising is one of the most remunerative employments."

Hops may be seen "growing thriftily and bearing abundantly." The State is "prolific in native dye-plants." In its forests abound "nearly every variety of tree known in the United States." For cattle raising it is perhaps the finest country of the world. Turn, therefore, in which direction we may, we find that nature has provided for that diversification of demand for human service for which we look in vain amid the fields of northern States. Seeking for it in these latter, we find ourselves compelled to look below the surface, and there alone; yet there it is that Massachusetts, anxious to protect her pin and pipe makers, insists that it shall not be sought.

The war has already made great changes, yet are they, as it would seem, but preliminary to greater in the future, as you will see by the paragraphs that follow :—

"Vast numbers of freedmen could be hired for one or two months at a time, for liberal day wages. This system is in conformity with their ideas and notions of work; they reluctantly contract for a year. Rye, barley and buckwheat have been tried in Louisiana. Barley and buckwheat are both natives of a southern climate, and flourish remarkably well here. *In Texas, during the past year, the papers state that eighty-five bushels of barley were made to the acre in Central Texas.* Sixty bushels could easily be made here, and as it is superior to the northern barley for brewing, the fourteen breweries of New Orleans would alone consume vast quantities of it. *Barley, as compared with corn, is a better food for stock, particularly work stock*, as it is muscle producing and does not heat the system like the oil or fat producing property of corn, *and while it produces three times as much to the acre, of grain, the stock consumes all of the straw.* A hand can cultivate much more ground in barley than corn, and it needs no working after planting. Grain growing would not only be profitable to the planter, but it would build up New Orleans, and make her the greatest city on the continent. What New Orleans lacks is a summer trade; her business has been heretofore compressed into six or eight months. After the cotton and sugar crops had been received and disposed of, the merchants and tradesmen had nothing to do. Most of them went North with their families, leaving New Orleans a prey to epidemics, when a small portion of the very money which they had earned in New Orleans, and were spending so lavishly abroad, would have perfected sanitary measures, which would have protected her from the epidemics. During this season of inactivity nearly all branches of business are suspended; the merchant must, however, pay house rent, insurance, clerk's hire and other incidental expenses; must lose interest on his investments, and have his goods and wares damaged by rust, dust, moth and mould. If the cultivation of grain were begun and encouraged around New Orleans, grain would pour in during the month of May, and the summer months, and would fill up this fatal hiatus in our trade.

"The merchant would be compelled to reside here in summer as well as winter, and he would be forced on his own account to lend his time and money towards building up the city and improving its health.

"Every branch of business would be kept up then throughout the whole year, and *our own steamships would supply the countries south of us with provisions, and we should not, as now, be compelled to import coffee by way of Cincinnati.* Northern and European emigrants, knowing that our grain growing was more profitable than at the North, and that *they could grow grain without working during the summer months in that sun they have been wrongfully taught to dread, would flock to our lands; and of course, where provisions and all other necessaries of life would be cheap, manufactures would necessarily spring up, to work up the raw materials so abundant here.* I have thus lengthily urged the cultivation of the cereals, because I find so little is known among the most intelligent, as to the capabilities of our State in this respect, and because, too, I think that therein lies the true secret of recuperation and permanent prosperity for our people. It is a business which all classes of agriculturists may profitably engage in, from the poor farmer of the pine hills to the rich planter of the coast. It is a business in which every landholder, lessee, laborer, mechanic, manufacturer, tradesman, merchant, ship-owner, and, indeed, every citizen, is deeply interested, as it is a question of large profits and cheap bread, and the State of Louisiana and the United States have a deep concern in it, as large owners of land in the State. I have placed grain first in the list of productions, for looking to the future, *I am sure that grain will become our leading staple, and that New Orleans is destined to become the leading grain market of the world.*"

Such being the Southern anticipations, the question now arises, are they likely to be realized? That you may yourself answer this question, I ask you now to look again at the West and North-west and see—

First, that as a consequence of that Massachusetts policy which requires that raw materials of every kind, coal, lead, and iron not excepted, shall be low in price, the West has thus far been wholly deprived of power to bring the miner and the manufacturer to the side of the farmer, and thus to relieve its producers from the burthensome and destructive tax of transportation.*

Second, that, as a necessary consequence of this, the powers of the soil have gradually diminished and are diminishing, with constantly increasing necessity for scattering over more widely extended surfaces, with steadily augmenting tax for commissions and for freights, and constantly increasing exposure to loss resulting from excess or deficiency of moisture, from excessive heat or cold.

---

* At the moment at which I write I find notice of sales of corn in Iowa at 8 cents per bushel, yet does the State abound in ores whose development would make demand for all the food that could be raised.

Nearly twenty years have now elapsed since the then head of the Patent Office, an eminent agriculturist, estimated our "annual waste" of the mineral constituents of corn, under the "cheap raw material" system, at the equivalent of 1,500,000,000 bushels of corn, and told the nation that if such "earth butchery" were continued, the hour would soon arrive when "the last throb of the nation would have ceased, and when America, Greece, and Rome would stand together among the ruins of the past." From that hour to the present, with but slight exception, we have moved in the same false direction, the result now exhibiting itself in the fact that the great West, the "granary of the world," has so little food to spare that the whole amount of our export is much less than is now required for payment of the mere interest upon debts contracted in Europe for cloth and iron that should have been made at home. This present season has been a fine one for the farmer, and for months past have we been assured that it would in a great degree compensate for the short harvests of the past two years; but the actual result now presents itself in the following passage from the *Tribune* of the day on which I write :—

"Advices from the West in regard to wheat are unsatisfactory. An extra yield has ceased to be talked about, and the fact is apparent that it threshes out poorly in comparison with the estimates before harvest. Measurement shows 12 and 14 bushels where 25 per acre were expected, and the increased breadth sown will scarcely make up for the deficit in yield. So far as wheat is concerned, cheap bread cannot be realized from the crop of 1867, nor are the prospects better for corn at the present moment. Already Western experts are buying old corn on speculation, paying $1 25 per bushel, against 83 cents in September, 1866. This state of things is in marked contrast with the general expectations forty days since, and will modify many business calculations then made. Instead of an abundant harvest of wheat and corn to make cheap bread, and consequently cheaper labor, high prices appear inevitable, with all the attendant disasters. Instead of a crop which would tax the rolling stock of railroads to their utmost, and enable them to clear their books of floating debt, managers are brought face to face with the fact that there is not an average crop, and that its transportation will yield little profit. To traders this changed appearance of the crop is of vital importance. Instead of a full crop to be used in the payment of old debts and in exchange for new commodities, producers from this year's labor promise to be left where old debts must be neglected, and new purchases made sparingly."

Need we desire better evidence than is here furnished that the raising of raw produce for the supply of distant markets is the proper work of the barbarian and the slave, and of those alone? I think not. Twenty years of the Massachusetts system—that one which claims for its own people all the protection they need, while denying it to the people of the Centre, the West, and the South—that one which refuses to "stimulate domestic competition" for the *purchase* of raw products, or the *sale* of finished ones—have sufficed for so reducing the power of the whole body of loyal States to maintain commerce with the outer world that *their whole exports, gold and bonds excepted, scarcely more than suffice for meeting the*

4

demands of Europe for interest and freights—leaving but little for payment even of the travelling expenses of our people, now amounting to scarcely less than $100,000,000 per annum.

The remedy for all this has been provided by nature, which has underlaid the soil with coal and ores, but Massachusetts wars upon the miner and thus compels the farmer still further to exhaust the soil by sending wool and corn in their rudest forms to distant markets, there to be exchanged for other wool and corn in the forms of cloth and iron.

At the South nature has provided for removal of all existing difficulties, having placed the farmer in such position that not only is he nearer to the great markets for his products in their original forms, but that he may convert his wheat and his sweet potatoes into cotton, into pork, oranges, or any other of the numerous fruits above referred to, for all of which he finds an outlet in the various markets of the world. Seeing these things, and seeing further, that its whole upland country presents one of the most magnificent climates of the world, can it be doubted that the day is at hand *when emigration to the South and Southwest must take the place now occupied by emigration to the West, and when power is to pass from the poor soils of the Northeast to those richer ones which now offer themselves in such vast abundance in the Centre, the South, and the Southwest?* As I think, it cannot. In my belief the time is fast approaching when northern intelligence will be everywhere found engaged in teaching southern men how they may be best enabled to square their long-running account with the men of Massachusetts; and when almost every town and village of the South will be found offering protection to the makers of pins and pipes, nails and bars, tubs and buckets, shoes and cloths, in the manner here described as having but now occurred in Maine :—

"The town of St. Albans, Somerset County, Me., recently voted to exempt from taxation, for the space of ten years, any sum not less than ten thousand dollars that might be invested in any permanent manufacturing business."

That such is now the tendency of the Southern mind is clearly obvious. Look where we may throughout the South and Southwest, we meet with evidence of the facts that their people have profited of the experience of the past few years, and that they now see the necessity for making themselves independent of the North. The Report now before me everywhere urges the development of the vast mineral resources of the country—the establishment of furnaces and forges—the erection of cotton-mills—and closes with a proposal for the establishment of a Bureau specially charged with carrying these ideas into full effect, and authorized to offer premiums to those who may engage therein. Such is now the feeling of every Southern State, and such will certainly be its course of action.

The day for all this is at hand. Is Massachusetts preparing for it? Is she making home so attractive as to lessen emigration? Is she not, on the contrary, under the "cheap raw material" system, now expelling more rapidly than ever before her native population, replacing it with one greatly inferior drawn from distant lands, and thus lowering the standard of all? Of this there can be no doubt whatsoever.

How may this be prevented in the future? How may she be enabled to maintain her position, prospering in common with the South, the West, and the Centre? To enable us to obtain the answer to this question let us now for a moment study the widely different policies of France and England.

The one has been engaged in *protecting* herself, never having warred upon the rival industries of other countries. To that end she has always sought, as she is now seeking, to place herself in the lead of the world as regards artistic development, and this is now as much exhibited in her iron works as it so long has been in the factories of Lyons and St. Etienne. Selling much skill, and but little raw material, she cares little how much this latter costs, and can, therefore, afford to permit the rest of the world to pursue the course of action that leads to freedom.

The other, on the contrary, has been steadily engaged, not only in preventing elsewhere the growth of diversification in the modes of employment, but in destroying it wherever it previously had existed. To that end she has been competing with the lowest priced labor of the world. Selling mere brute force, and much raw material, she cares greatly about the cost of this latter; and, in the effort to cheapen it, she has become the promoter of slavery, whether black, white, or brown, in every region of the world. Her words, like those of Massachusetts, are words of freedom, but her policy, again like that of Massachusetts, is that which tends to put the whip in the hands of the slave-driver, whether in the bank or on the farm, in the factory or on the plantation, be the color of the slave what it may.

The one becomes from day to day more independent of the tariff regulations of the world. The other becomes from hour to hour more dependent, and hence it is that she now seeks so anxiously to make amends for her discreditable conduct during the recent war. Hence, too, it is that she now pays so liberally all the men amongst ourselves, home grown and foreign, who employ themselves in teaching our people the *advantage* to be derived from tearing out and exporting the soil, and carrying it thousands of miles over lands so filled with coal and iron ore that the match thereto can be found in no other country of the world.

Of these two policies, the one tending towards elevation of the laborer, the other toward his depression—the one toward national independence, the other toward national dependence — which is it that has thus far been followed by Massachusetts? Is it not the "cheap raw material" one—that one which tends towards subjugation of the laborer and perpetuation of the national dependence ? That it is so cannot be questioned, nor can it be doubted that it is in this direction we must look if we desire to find the cause of the change now occurring in reference to the character of her population. Let that change go on as it now is going, and the day will not be distant when she will find that her day of power is over, and that she must be content to take her place among the great trading communities of the past. Holland was once all powerful, but the hour is now at hand when she will take her proper place as merely one of the provinces of the great Germanic Empire.

Desiring to retain her place in the Union, Massachusetts should at once awake to the fact that her policy has been selfish and illiberal, and that it can end nowhere but in ruin. Let her then promptly recognize the existence of a harmony of interests among all the portions of the Union, and let her see that the more the southern people can be led to convert their cotton into yarns and cloth the greater must be the demand upon her for those finer goods she may so soon be prepared to furnish. Let her follow in the train of France, making demand for taste and brains instead of muscle, and she will then retain her native population. By that course, *and that alone*, will she be enabled to retain her influence, and to regain, in the commerce of the world, that position which, under the " cheap raw material" system, she has to so great an extent already lost.

She has been long engaged in making bitter enemies, and they abound in nearly every quarter of the Union. Let her now, by manifesting a *real* love for freedom, a *real* love for the Union, a *really* national spirit, seek to convert those enemies into friends. Fully believing that if she fail so to do she will herself be the greatest sufferer, I remain

Yours faithfully,

HENRY C. CAREY.

Hon. HENRY WILSON.

PHILADELPHIA, Sept., 1867.

LETTER ELEVENTH.

DEAR SIR :—

Seeking to obtain financial reconstruction we must begin by an industrial one, it being wholly impossible that we should ever again avail ourselves of the services of the precious metals so long as our commercial policy shall continue to impose upon us a necessity for not only exporting the whole produce of California, but of sending with it gold-bearing bonds to the annual extent of almost hundreds of millions of dollars. In like manner must both industrial and financial reconstruction precede the political one that is to have any, even the slightest, chance of permanence. The former are the bases on which the latter must rest, and therefore is it that I so much regret your having in your Address so wholly excluded both from notice.

The industrial question having been now to some extent examined, although not by any means exhausted, I propose next to ask your attention to the financial one, as follows :—

In speaking of the currency it is usual to refer to that portion of it only which takes the form of circulating notes, leaving wholly out of view that which exists in the shape of credits to individuals on the books of banks, and which have been, and always must be, the real causes of financial crises. By a recent report now before me of the condition of the national banks, the amount of those credits was about $500,000,000, the whole of which large sum, with the exception of about $100,000,000 remaining in bank vaults in the form of specie or legal tender notes, had been lent out and was then bearing interest. The difference, $400,000,000, constituted the currency created by banks, and liable at any moment to contraction, at the will of bank directors.

Again, the daily creation of currency in those forms in which it comes before the clearing houses, amounts, in this city and New York alone, to more than $30,000,000.

The persons chiefly contributing to the creation of this latter form of currency number by hundreds, and with many of them the daily amount counts by hundreds of thousands. In like manner some few hundreds of persons control institutions to which the country stands indebted for the former, and thus it is that we obtain what may properly be characterized as the *aristocratic* form of currency creation ; that form which seems most to please our legislators and our finance ministers, as, not only do they wholly fail to inquire into the expediency of leaving so much power in the hands of private individuals, but *to them*, precisely, is it that they always look for advice as to the further measures needed to be pursued. The shepherd thus asks of the wolf how he may best provide for the safety of his sheep, the wolf giving for answer precisely such advice as promises most to enable him to gobble up the flock with comfort to himself.

For the poor sheep there is provided a currency which takes the tangible form of circulating notes ; that one by means of which the shop-keeper is enabled promptly to pay the farmer, the workman to pay the shop-keeper, the employer at once to pay his workmen, and the merchant to pay on the instant the manufacturer. This is the *democratic* form of currency, and therefore is it that it has been always so much vituperated by that sham-democracy which has clamored so loudly in behalf of hard money and British free-trade. It is, too, that form in which it is being now maligned by that portion of the republican party which so much believes in maintaining protection at that point precisely which seems best to suit the purposes of Massachusetts, as nowhere "stimulating domestic competition" for the purchase of those raw products she needs to buy, or for the sale of those finished ones she needs to sell. In this she is doing little more than imitating the action of that democracy of the past which has so frequently sought the prohibition of notes below ten or twenty dollars, and has so uniformly ended by bringing about impoverishment of the people, the ruin of merchants, the stoppage of banks, the repudiation of State debts, the creation of *shin-plasters*, and the almost utter bankruptcy of the national treasury itself.

The years previous to the war were, throughout the West and South, marked by an exaggeration of the almost ruinous state of things by which the crisis of '57 had been attended. The farmer, desiring to sell his potatoes, his fruits, his corn, was required to accept "store pay," or retain his produce on his hands unsold. The miner, in like manner, was required to accept "orders" on store-keepers who fixed prices to suit themselves. The little Western farmer, desiring to mortgage his farm to obtain the means with which to improve it, was required to pay two or three per cent. per month, or even more. Everybody was in debt, not from want of property, but because of the absence of any medium of circulation by aid of which the coal operator and the farmer could be enabled to pay the store-keeper, and the latter to buy for cash in the cities with which he dealt.

The war gave us in the "green-back" the machinery by means of which labor could promptly be exchanged for food and fuel, cloth and iron, and at once all was changed. Forthwith the societary circulation became rapid, and with every step of progress in that direction the nation acquired strength. To the tariff of '61, to the "greenback," and to the State in which I write, have we been indebted for power to make the war, and therefore, perhaps, it is, that the whole period of peace has been characterized by an incessant war upon them, each and all.

Next in order came the establishment of a national banking system, in itself a good measure, but so very bad in its details that, if they be not corrected, it must inevitably bring about a separation of the trading States of the North and East from the producing States of the Centre, West, and South.

Requiring a deposit of the whole capital as security for redemption of the circulation, it throws the banks on circulation and deposits for power to perform the services for which they were intended. Taxing them heavily it thus produces a necessity for over-trading, and for thus causing that inflation of which our eastern friends so much complain, but which they will be the last to remedy, for the reason that they themselves so largely profit by it. By a recent statement now before me, the joint capital of the national banks is shown to be . . . $418,000,000 while the amount of their interest-bearing investments is . . . . 1,122,000,000 thus closely approaching three to one.

Turn back now, I pray you, twenty years, and study the operations of the banks in your own vicinity, those which have most freely furnished circulation, and have most uniformly met their obligations. Doing this, you will find that while the loans of Rhode Island institutions rarely exceeded their capitals to the extent of *a third*, those of your own State rarely went beyond *a half*, or fifty per cent. In both, the banking system presented true pyramids, with elevation that was slight in proportion to their bases; whereas, the national one gives us an inverted pyramid the greatest breadth of which is found in the air, and which may, therefore, be readily toppled over.

Why is this so? Because this latter is *a great money monopoly*, for the especial benefit of the Trading States. Limiting the amount of circulation to $200,000,000, it by that means limits the capital to be applied to the great money trade—*the most important of all trades:* and does so for the reason that outside of the cities the deposits are so very trifling in amount.

A monopoly having been thus created, we may now inquire who they are that profit by it. Doing this, we find that the Eastern States, with perhaps a twelfth of the population, have had granted to them above a third of this monopoly power; that New York, with an eighth of the population, has almost a fourth; that this State, with a population nearly as large as that of New England, has been limited to little more than an eighth; that to Ohio, Indiana, and Illinois, with a population far more than twice as great as that of New England, there has been allowed little more than a third as much; and, that for the vast region beyond the Mississippi and south of the Delaware and the Ohio—containing more than two-fifths of our population—there has been allowed *just one-ninth;* or less than is *daily manufactured* in New York and Philadelphia.

Do the people of New England, my dear sir, find that they have too much of the machinery of circulation? Do those of New York? Do they not, on the contrary, frequently complain that the notes cannot be found that are needed for the work to be performed? How then must it be with this State whose needs have been supplied to but little more than a third of those of the New England States? How must it be with Ohio and her immediate neighbors? How, above all, must it be with the almost thirty States and territories that with a present population *four times as great* as that of New England, are allowed banking powers and privileges *less than a third* as great.

The money shop is denied them. The power to create local circulation of any kind is denied them. Pressed thus to the wall, one southern city made an effort to provide for enabling its own people to make exchanges with each other, but then down came Congress with a tax of, I think, ten per cent. upon such local circulation. In this manner it is, my dear sir, that our northern and eastern friends, luxuriating in their full supply of banks and circulating notes, are furnishing the "warm and generous greeting" of which you so recently have spoken.

As a consequence of this it is, that New York and New England are now enabled to lend circulating notes on the best security, at the south, at two per cent. per month; and that southern people now pay, regularly, three, four, five, and even, as it has been stated, ten per cent. per month, for the use of little pieces of paper issued by northern and eastern banks for the private profit of their stockholders. Such *may* be the road to permanent reconstruction, but if it is, I, for one, must say, that it does not so to my mind present itself. Bad as is all this, we are promised that it shall, for the unfortunate people outside of the Trading States, yet be worse. Up to this time they have had the advantage of some portion of the "green-back" circulation, but of that they are, as our Finance Minister insists, to be gradually, but certainly deprived. The circulation, as he gravely assures us, is quite too large, and contraction is to be, as he so long has desired that we should understand it must be, the order of the day. This the West resists, and moves the House that further strengthening of the money monopoly of the trading States, New York and New England, be dispensed with. The vote being taken, but sixty-five votes are found adverse to the motion, and of these there are from

New England and New York 38
All other States 27

Total 65

The majority, favorable to the doctrine of equal rights among the States, numbers 95
Of these there are from

New England and New York 13
All others 82

The vote for the resolution outside of the Trading States is therefore more than three to one. Were the question now to be taken, it is doubtful if even a single adverse vote could be found south or west of those States. Outside of them the treasury system has scarcely a friend. Why should it have? In no country of the world is the supply of currency so small when compared with the commerce for whose service it is needed.

Of the "green-backs" the amount at present existing is but $370,000,000
Of national bank-notes there are less than . . 300,000,000

$670,000,000

Of these the quantity always in bank, or in the treasury, and thus out of circulation, is never less than 170,000,000

Leaving but . . $500,000,000

for the service of nearly 40,000,000, scattered over a whole continent. Of this the little New England has, legal tenders included, more than a fourth, leaving the balance for the service of the less fortunate portion of our population. One of two things is certain: either New England has thrice too much, or the rest of the country much too little. The former does not think she has more than she needs, and will relinquish none. Neither will she agree to any increase elsewhere. On the contrary her people, in and out of Congress, lecture the unfortunates who have not the happiness of residing east of the Hudson, after the following fashion :—.

"If the people of this country could be made to see that the present expanded currency is not a blessing but a curse ; that it is one of the most unequal and burdensome of taxes ; that it gives undue value to capital as compared with labor, thus pressing most heavily on the working classes, tending to make the rich richer and the poor poorer ; that it stimulates speculation (which is gambling under a less offensive name) by turning the most active and ambitious men from the occupations of production to those of exchange, from mechanics and farmers into brokers and middle-men ; that it drives men from the country into the cities, in the hope of sudden wealth, and because it is thought more respectable to buy and to sell than to labor with the hands ; that it subverts all true notions of value and produces such constant fluctuations as to make honest industry insecure of its rewards ; if the people can be made to see all these evils, and will open their eyes to the enervating, demoralizing consequences, they will patiently and cheerfully submit to the temporary hardships which are involved in reducing this redundant currency to its normal proportions ; they will by all their influence strengthen the hands of Congress and of the Secretary of the Treasury, that the day may be hastened when this country shall again conduct its domestic and foreign dealings on the basis of the only currency which can render trade secure—that of the precious metals."

The author of this, my dear sir, is one of your own constituents—one of those who, in common with the rest of the New England people, have secured for themselves a fixed and certain allowance of currency more than three times greater than is, by law, now allowed to nearly thirty States and Territories, with a population five times greater, and standing greatly more in need of tangible machinery of circulation. Do you, however, find in it any suggestion that the monopoly now existing shall be in any manner modified; that the power already obtained over the currency shall in any way be lessened? Not in the least. It says to the Centre, the South, and the West, surrender a part of the little we have left you, and let our monopoly be rendered more complete, and more than this it does not say.

The day, however, for all this is past. Massachusetts must determine voluntarily to abandon the idea of manufacturing, money, and trading monopolies, or she will raise such a storm in the Centre, the West, and the South, as will compel her so to do. Fully believing this, and as much believing it to be the duty of Pennsylvania, as Keystone and Guardian of the Union to take the lead in a movement to that end, I remain,

Yours very truly,

HENRY C. CAREY.

Hon. H. Wilson.

Philadelphia, September, 1867.

LETTER TWELFTH.

Dear Sir :—

The Fort Wayne decree of Secretary McCulloch, likely to prove of far more enduring importance than the Berlin and Milan decrees of the Emperor Napoleon, is now nearly two years old. As it stands it constitutes the great financial blunder of the age, having already, by the paralysis of which it has been the cause, cost the country more than the whole amount of the national debt. Let its policy be persevered in and it will constitute the greatest in history, for *it will have cost the Union its existence.*

Gladly hailed by the capitalists and bankers of your State, and by the gentlemen who represent them in Congress, *contraction* has, from that day to the present, been the burden of their song. What, however, was it that they desired to see contracted ? Any portion of the $100,000,000 of circulation that they had so promptly appropriated to their own especial use ? Any part of the $170,000,000 appropriated by the combined Trading States, New York and New England ? Certainly not. That for whose *contraction* they have since so loudly clamored constituted nearly the whole machinery of exchange throughout the Producing States with their present population of 30,000,000, likely very soon to be 50,000,000. For these, their unfortunate *subjects*, there was to be allowed in all the future the fixed amount of $130,000,000, or, even now, but *four dollars* per head; the compact New England, whose need, per head, for some tangible medium of circulation, was not one-half as great, meanwhile luxuriating in a circulation of *thirty* dollars per head, and finding even that not to be at all in excess of its actual wants.

On a former occasion, as you may recollect, it was shown that your State, in its anxiety for commercial reform, had magnanimously and liberally offered to the West, in exchange for what it claimed to need, a surrender of the rights of its late allies of the Mining Centre. What then was done has now been repeated here, her anxiety for financial reform having led her to insist upon a total surrender of the rights of the Producing States, and the member for Lynn having uniformly taken the lead in insisting that such surrender should be made. A monopoly of the money power had been obtained, and it was to be maintained even at the cost of reducing the whole people of the Producing States, loyal or disloyal, to the condition here described as now existing in the Mormon State :—

59

"Wheat is the usual legal tender of the country. Horses, harness, vehicles, cattle, and hay are cash; eggs, butter, pistols, knives, stockings, and whiskey are change; pumpkins, potatoes, sorghum molasses, and calves are 'shinplasters,' which are taken at a discount, and with which the Saints delight to pay their debts (if it is ever a delight to pay debts). Business in this community, with this currency, is a very curious and amusing pastime. A peddler, for instance, could take out his goods in a carpet-bag, but would need a 'bull' train to freight back his money. I knew a man who refused an offer to work in the country at fifty dollars a month because he would need a forty-hundred wagon and four yoke of oxen to haul his week's wages to the whiskey-shop, theatre, &c., on Saturday evening. * * * When a man once lays out his money in any kind of property, it is next to impossible to reconvert it into money. There is many a man here who, when he first came into the valley, had no intention of remaining but a short time, but soon got so involved that he could never get away without making heavy pecuniary sacrifices. Property is a Proteus, which you must continue to grip firmly, notwithstanding his slippery changes, until you have him in his true shape. Now you have him as a fine horse and saddle: presto, he is only sixty gallons of sorghum molasses; now he changes into two cows and a calf, and before you have time to think he is transformed into fifteen cords of wood up in the mountain canon; next he becomes a yoke of oxen; then a 'shutler' wagon; ha! is he about to slip from you at last in the form of bad debts?"

Place, I pray you, the people of Massachusetts in this position, and determine for yourself how they would think and *act*. Study the picture, for it is a tolerably accurate one of that which now prevails throughout a large portion of the Centre, South, and West.

To the hour at which was issued that most unfortunate and ill-advised decree there had still remained in existence most of that *faith in the future* by means of which we had been carried safely through the war. From that hour it began to pass away, and with each successive day there has been seen an increased desire to *centralize* in the trading cities the disposable capital of the country—hoarding with banks and bankers, trust and deposit companies, at small interest, the means that otherwise would have been employed in opening mines, building furnaces, mills, or ships, mining coal, or making cloth. From that unfortunate hour works of national importance were abandoned, mills and factories commenced to contract their operations, coal tended more and more to become a drug in the market, and the demand for labor to decline. From that hour money tended to accumulate in all those cities, and to become more and more inaccessible to men by which it could be made to create demand for human service. From that hour the poor tended to become poorer and the rich to become richer, till, as now, the Boston capitalist obtains twice the war rate of interest, the little Western farmer, as is shown by the following passage from a money article of the day on which I write, meanwhile gradually returning to the enormous rates of the period before the war:—

"At the West rates of interest are, as usual, far in advance of our home figures. *An agency has been established in Boston, within a very short time, for negotiating first-class Western mortgages at ten per centum.* In Cincinnati the bank depositors have to pay from eight to nine per centum, and the lowest street rate is ten per cent. Two per cent. a month is not a very uncommon figure out West. In the southwest the rates of interest would appear enormous to even the eyes of the sharpest Eastern note-shaver. *In Memphis three to five per centum a month are common figures."—Press.*

Such being the state of things in the green wood, what will it be in the dry? When the Secretary made his speech denunciatory of the best currency the people had ever had, the legal-tenders stood at . . . . . · . . . $400,000,000
On the first of last month we had . . . 369,164,344
                                                                ──────────
Reduction in 22 months $30,835,156

There are yet, therefore, to be withdrawn nearly $370,000,000. When that shall have been done may we not hope to hear of agencies in the Eastern States for negotiating first-class Western mortgages at more than double the rate above described? That we shall do so, I feel quite assured.

The money monopoly already here established is, I am well satisfied, the worst at present in existence in any country claiming to rank as civilized; yet is it now seriously proposed to make it from day to day more complete, and thus to establish a subjection to the money power of our whole people, black and white, without a parallel in financial history.

We are, however, gravely told that it is in this manner alone that we are to be enabled to return to the use of the precious metals. What has been our progress in that direction, in two years of paralysis throughout which the Secretary has been unremitting in his efforts at contraction, will be seen on an examination of the following figures, representing millions of dollars :—

	Oct. 1865.	Oct. 1866.	July, 1867.
Banking capital . . .	393	403	418
Interest-bearing investments .	1,020	1,060	1,122

Twenty-five millions have thus been added to the base, a hundred meanwhile to the superstructure, and the edifice having more and more assumed the form of an inverted pyramid that may at any moment be toppled over. So must it continue to do for every hour of the future in which the McCulloch-Massachusetts system shall continue to be maintained, the direct effect of paralysis being that of giving increased power to banks and bankers, and all others of the class which controls and regulates that portion of the currency which has been designated as *aristocratic*, and from which our crises always have come and must always come.

To the $100,000,000 of the incorporated banks may now, as I doubt not, be added half as much, additional to the quantity that had been usually controlled by individuals, and by institutions other than banks, in those war days when the public policy tended to favor those who had money to borrow and labor to sell, instead of, as now, favoring those who have money to sell and labor to buy. *That $150,000,000, centralized in the few trading cities, does more to produce that which it is the fashion of the day to call inflation than would be done by fire times the amount of greenbacks scattered among the 30,000,000 of people inhabiting the Producing States.*

By its help it is that money is made cheap to the British iron-master who places his products in the public stores, while made so dear to the coal-miner that he becomes bankrupt by reason of inability to borrow at two per cent. per month. By its means the country is flooded with foreign iron requiring for its payment $2,000,000 per month of California gold. By its means our people are being from hour to hour more compelled to look to the large cities as the only places at which exchanges can be made, and the more they are so compelled the higher becomes the taxation of the Producing States for maintenance of owners of New York and Boston hotels and houses. The higher that taxation, and the poorer the people of the Producing States, the greater becomes the ability of owners of city property to live abroad, and thus to swell the amount of *travelling bills* that have already reached so high a figure as to require for their payment a sum equal to nearly the whole amount of the exports of the loyal States, leaving little beyond gold and bonds with which to pay for foreign merchandise consumed at home. Study carefully these facts, my dear sir, and you will find little difficulty in understanding how it is that the Massachusetts policy is now compelling us to go abroad to borrow money, on the security of the State, at almost thrice the rate of interest paid by Britain.

According to Mirabeau, "capitals are necessities, but," as he added, "when the head grows too large the body becomes apoplectic and wastes away."—British free-trade, and Massachusetts determination to resist any measure tending to promote "domestic competition," have combined to make of the little territory east of the Hudson a head so large that we are threatened with precisely the state of things above described. The "waste" is now going on, and, unless the system be resisted, must so increase as to produce financial, moral, and political death; that, too, despite all your efforts at political reconstruction.

Prices, however, it is insisted, must be reduced. So were we told two years since by men who did not trouble themselves to study the fact that years were needed for enabling us to restore our stock of hogs and cattle, cows and horses, even to the point at which it had stood before the war. So are we now told by others who do not care to see that constant exhaustion of the soil of the West and Northwest has made our supplies of food more precarious than they had ever been before.* That some prices must

* The average quantity of certain articles that passed the New York canals in the three seasons 1848, 1849, and 1850, closely following the

have been reduced is shown by statements of the *Tribune* in reference to the number of persons now wholly unemployed in New
York city. That others have been reduced you may find on visit-
ing our mining region, where men who are not wholly unemployed
are compelled to accept half war prices in return for labor, while
paying almost war prices for the food consumed by their families
and themselves. Petroleum has become so complete a drug that
most of the wells have been abandoned, and the men who therein
had been used to labor have been dismissed. Cotton, by reason
of the closing of our mills, has been piled up in Liverpool until
it, too, threatens to become as great a drug as it had been in the
good old British free-trade times when British manufacturers could
pick and choose at five pence. Contraction is, throughout the
Producing States, putting down the price of American labor and
its products, while putting up the prices of money, cotton cloth,
and various other things that Massachusetts has to sell, yet has
the process but begun. It is carrying into full effect the idea that,
so far as I am informed, was first broached in the Newport Convention twenty years since, that "domestic competition" must be
prevented, whether for purchase of raw materials or sale of finished
goods ; and with the further addition, that there is not in the
future to be allowed, throughout the Producing States, any competition with the trading States for the sale of money. The
monopoly of that important trade is now in the hands of these
latter; and that it is to be rigorously maintained has been proved
by Massachusetts action throughout the last Congress.

The tax on cotton being specific, the lower the price the more
burthensome does it become. The McCulloch-Massachusetts
policy has largely reduced its price while doubling the rate of
interest paid by its producer, yet is the tax collected. Such
being one of the "warm and generous greetings" extended to our
erring brethren of the South, the question now arises as to how
many such will be required for producing resistance in a form
that, when it shall come, *as come it must*, will result in perfect
achievement of the object.

Taxes are heavy. Collected in the Trading States, they are
finally paid in those Producing States to which it is now proposed
to allow a circulation of *four dollars* per head, the people of New
England meanwhile jealously retaining their *thirty dollars* per

passage of the pro-slavery tariff of 1846, and in the first half of the present
and the past seasons, is as follows :—

	Seasons of 1848, '49, '50.	Half seasons, May 1 to July 31, 1865, '66, '67.
Flour, barrels	3,224,000	148,000
Wheat, bushels	3,126,000	1,500,000
Corn, "	3,700,000	4,300,000
Pork, barrels	69,000	5,000
Beef, "	87,000	2,400

In that time the population, chiefly occupied in tearing out and exporting
the soil, must have more than quintupled.

head, and lending out the surplus to the Centre, South, and West at prices varying, as we see, between ten and fifty per cent. per annum. Moving in this direction, how long, my dear sir, will it be before we shall attain a perfect reconstruction? Shall we not sooner reach a new rebellion? I think we shall.

Throughout the war we were steadily congratulated on the facts, that the certificates of public debt were nearly all held at home—that the number of small bond-holders was immense—that we had thus an important security for punctual payment of the interest. Since the peace all this, however, has been changed, the great object now sought by the Treasury, and by our Massachusetts friends, to be attained, being low prices for human service and for all the rude products of mining and agricultural labor. The lower those prices the greater becomes the necessity for selling the little fifty dollar bond in which had been invested the savings of a year, and the greater the centralization of certificates of public debt in the hands of Eastern and European capitalists. Going ahead under the McCulloch-Massachusetts system, the time must soon arrive when nine-tenths, or more, of this interest will need to be paid north and east of Pennsylvania, in the Trading States and in Europe; the Producing States meanwhile paying nearly all the public taxes, and thereto adding two, three, if not even five, per cent. per month, for the use of circulating notes so liberally allowed to our New England friends. Should this system be maintained, might it not lead to non-payment of the interest? I think it would.

On occasion of the dedication of the Gettysburg Cemetery, Mr. Lincoln declared that this was " a government of the people, by the people, and for the people;" and in this most of my fellow-citizens of the Centre are in full accord with him. They do *not* believe that it is a government of the Centre, the West, and the South, by the North and East, and for the special benefit of the trading States. Well will it be for the people of these latter if they can at an early date arrive at the conclusion that Mr. Lincoln had been right and that their whole policy, directly opposed thereto as it has been, had been a most unwise one !

Mr. McCulloch's policy has been one great mistake, and it has proved a most costly failure. Seeing, that the law had created a monopoly of the money power; that while it limited the base of the edifice it set no limit to the elevation; that with every hour it was becoming more top-heavy and more in danger of being toppled over; seeing all this, I say, he should have asked of Congress an extension to the people of the Producing States of all those powers which had been so fully granted to the trading ones, and he should have then encouraged the creation of local institutions for the service of the 30,000,000 of people who are now so unjustly, and unconstitutionally, made mere hewers of wood and drawers of water for their brethren of the northeast. So doing, he would have prevented that accumulation of capital in trading centres which has been so freely used for speculation in commodities of first necessity, to the heavy loss of those by whom they were needed. So doing, he would have been aiding in the construction of mills and furnaces, and in the cheapening of cloth and iron. So doing, he would have made a home market for the hundreds of millions of bonds that have already gone to Europe, each new bank becoming a holder thereof to the whole extent of its circulation. So doing, he would have tied the States together, and would have been bringing about the "more perfect union" that we had all so much desired. Not having so done, he has brought about a state of things so purely sectional that it must, *and should*, provoke resistance.

At this moment circulating notes are very scarce in Eastern cities. Why? Because of the help demanded by their poor clients of the South and West for movement of their very little crops. Why, however, cannot the Producing States help themselves? Why not, like Massachusetts, *make* such notes? Why, bone and sinew of the country, and ultimate payers of nearly all the taxes, as they certainly are, should they be held in such complete dependence? Because they are being made mere puppets whose strings are to be pulled at their master's pleasure! To make the thing complete, it is now required only, that the "greenback" be annihilated, and that all banks south and west of the Hudson be required, as it is meant they shall be, to place in New York City lawful money with which to redeem their notes. Thereafter, the wolves may, at their entire convenience, devour the poor and unfortunate sheep, *as it is proposed they shall do.*

More than any other State is Pennsylvania representative of the 30,000,000 of the Producing States: more than with any other, therefore, is it for her, in the existing state of things, to study her rights and her duties. So doing, she finds that to herself she owes it to insist that her citizens be placed on a precise equality with those of the Eastern States. To the Centre generally, to the South, Southwest, and West, she owes it to *demand* for them now, as in all the past she has done, the enjoyment of all the rights and privileges she claims for her people and herself. To the whole Union she owes it to *demand* the abandonment of that monopoly system which now threatens to defeat all efforts at reconstruction. To the world at large she owes it to interpose in behalf of the impoverished Southern people, and more especially of those colored men who are now threatened with a money tyranny more injurious in its effects than the slavery from which they have but now been rescued.

Such are her duties. That they will be performed I feel well assured. Fully believing that you, were you one of her citizens, would desire that they should be so, I remain

Yours, very truly,

HENRY C. CAREY.

HON. H. WILSON.

PHILADELPHIA, September, 1867.

LETTER THIRTEENTH—AND LAST.

Dear Sir :—

England believes in buying raw materials at low prices and selling finished goods at high ones. It is her *one* Article of Faith; that one her belief in which has brought about a necessity for reconstruction at home and abroad, in England herself and all her dependencies. France, under the imperial regime, has been following in the British footsteps, with daily growing necessity for a reconstruction the day for which cannot be now remote. Both are declining in influence, and thus are furnishing new evidence of the fleeting character of trading power. Our trading States take Britain for their model; and so rapid is their progress in the false direction that, while still dreaming of *reconstruction*, they are already face to face with a *dissolution* which, if allowed to come to pass, will prove a permanent one.

Germany and Russia, producing States, desire that raw materials should be high in price and finished commodities cheap. So do our Centre, South, and West. Natural allies of the two advancing countries of Europe, our fast friends throughout the war, these latter may safely leave the Trading States to their alliance with those declining ones which so gladly gave their countenance to the rebellion, and which now so clearly see that maintenance of their own political power is dependent wholly upon preventing permanent reconstruction here.

The tendencies of the two portions of the Union are thus, as we see, in opposite directions, and most especially must this be so now that the war has on one side *removed* the obstacle that had prevented combined action, while on the other it has *created* trading, manufacturing, and moneyed monopolies of fearful power. Can they in any manner be brought to act together? Will the Trading States cordially ally themselves with the Producing ones for the gradual, but certain, abolition of these monopolies? Will they agree upon a system that shall promote, and not prohibit, " domestic competition"? Upon the answer to be given to these questions now hangs the determination as to whether we are, or are not, to have a permanent political reconstruction embracing the whole of the existing States.

Prior to the Chicago Convention of 1860 it had, as I have already said, been determined by the Trading States that the platform, like that of 1856, should be confined to politics alone, leaving wholly unexpressed the desires of the people in reference to national questions of high importance. It was a British free-trade

5

plot, well arranged, but the defeat it met was thorough beyond example. From that time to the present the Republican party, in imitation of the old Democratic one, has been playing fast and loose with the question then decided, advocating British free-trade in one State and American free-trade in another; and so, as I just now read, it is proposed that it shall continue to do in all the future. The arrangements for all this are, as I doubt not, very perfect, but *the scheme will fail.* Of that you may rest assured. The next convention, like that of 1860, will find itself compelled either to indorse or repudiate the monopolies of which I have spoken; to be for or against the doctrine of equal rights; to be American or English; to be for or against that industrial independence without which any attempt at financial or political reconstruction is a useless waste of time and words. In 1860, men who had to that time been strenuous advocates of British free-trade and industrial dependence, found themselves compelled to join in the tumultuous demonstrations of joy at the reading of that resolution by which the party placed itself on the side of American independence. So, I feel confident, will it be again. Powerful as are the Trading States, there will, on that occasion, be found not even a single man so poor as to do reverence to the monopolies that the war has given us, or has so much strengthened.

Such is my firm belief, yet it may prove that the Trading States exercise a greater amount of influence than I anticipate, and that the advocates of high freights, dear money, dear cloth, and cheap raw materials, whether "wool or hemp, coal or iron," succeed in obtaining an indorsement of the policy of Massachusetts capitalists. Admitting now, for a moment, that such should be the case, what, in your opinion, would be the course of the people of your State were they to be at once transferred to the hills and valleys of Pennsylvania? Might they not, do you think, be disposed to invite *a Conference of the Producing States?* Might they not, in that invitation, show that the Trading States had had but one end in view, that of compelling the producing ones to make all their exchanges through the ports of New York and Boston, and through the mills of Old and New England? Might they not show that to the trading monopoly which had so long existed there had now been added a monopoly of the money power by means of which its holders had already become enabled to tax, almost at discretion, the people of the Producing States? Might they not show that every effort was now being made so to strengthen that monopoly as to render it tenfold more oppressive than as yet it had become? Might they not show that while the real wealth and strength of the country was to be found in the Producing States, their agents, the merely Trading States, had now become so confident as to have ventured to defy resistance? That done, might they not proceed to say—

That throughout a large portion of the Producing States, but most especially in the South and Southwest, there existed a wealth of soil, and a mineral wealth, without parallel in the world :

That what was needed for the development of both was population :

That immigration had always grown with great rapidity in periods of protection, while it had always decreased in those of British free-trade :

That to enable the people of Europe readily to reach the rich lands of the Centre, the South, and the West, it was indispensable that their owners should themselves be enabled freely to communicate with the whole outside world through the various ports that fringe the coast from the Delaware to the Rio Grande :

That to enable northern people to pass from the now exhausted lands of the West and Northwest, and thus obtain power to participate with their owners in the development of rich Southern lands, it was indispensable that roads should be made leading North and South, and not, as now, exclusively East and West :

That to the end that such roads might be made, and such ports be used, it was indispensable that measures should be adopted for enabling Southern and Western men to mine their own coal, smelt their own ores, and make their own cloth :

. That the one great object always held in view by the Trading States had been that of preventing, throughout the South and West, the application of capital and labor to the work of manufacture, and thus preventing any growth of "domestic competition" for either the purchase of raw materials or the sale of cloth :

That to the trading and manufacturing monopolies which had so long existed there had now been added a money monopoly of fearful power; one whose continued maintenance could have no result other than that of making the people of the Producing States mere hewers of wood and drawers of water for those who had so long been employed in forcing themselves into the position of being their exclusive agents :

That the real power was in their own hands, and that it rested wholly with themselves to determine whether their exchanges should in future be performed in the cities north of the Delaware or south of it :

That the time had arrived for exercise of that power, and that by the adoption of proper measures they could, if they would, compel the transfer to the South and West of a large portion of the machinery now in use in the Trading States :

That to the end of arriving at some clear understanding by means of which the Producing States should be enabled to establish an equality of rights; to secure to themselves free communication with the outer world; to obtain for themselves a proper supply of the machinery of circulation; to be freed from the present ruinous charges for the use of circulating notes; to proceed peacefully and quietly in the development of the vast resources placed by nature within their reach; to obtain that real freedom of trade which can exist in no country that exports raw produce; to establish that diversity in the demand for human service by means of which, alone, can the freedman be enabled to profit by the act of emancipation; and, finally, to secure that the Union, when reconstructed, shall be permanent; this conference had been invited.

Having read the above, allow me, once again, to ask that you place yourself and your constituents in the position of the people of Pennsylvania, feeling yourselves the proper representatives of great national interests whose development in other countries has brought wealth to the people and power to the State. Study then with them the history of our past legislation, and see how little creditable have been the influences, foreign and domestic, that have prevented such development. Study with them the consequences, and see that our supplies of food become more and more irregular as we become more dependent on other nations for cloth and iron. Study with them our monetary system, and see that nearly all the power that the States at large have lost has now become closely monopolized and mainly held in a few trading States. Study with them the results that even thus far have been realized, and then see with them that the strengthening of that monopoly, now so strongly urged, must result in grinding to powder the whole people of the Centre, the South, and the West. Study all these things, and then, I pray you, answer to yourself the question as to whether you would or would not, under such circumstances, hold that you would be failing in your duty to them, to the nation, and to the cause of civilization, if you did not strongly urge the adoption of the course of action that has above been indicated. That you would I feel well assured.

Will it, you may ask, be adopted? If so, will Pennsylvania find herself among allies or enemies?

To the first I confidently answer in the affirmative. To the second, that, unlike Massachusetts, Pennsylvania has no enemies.

Penn and his successors had a great mission on this Western Continent which, thus far, has been well performed. First to provide by legislative action for emancipation of the colored race, they simultaneously with New York emancipated the weaker sex from the Common Law tyranny in regard to rights to property. First to recognize the perfect equality of the States, large and small, they, in effect, made our present Union. Occupying a frontier State, and the only one liable to invasion, they stood, materially and politically, the bulwark of that Union throughout the late rebellion.— The crowning act yet remains to be performed, in now interposing between the Trading and Producing States for the purpose of bringing about that harmony of action without which the Union neither can, nor *ought to be*, maintained; and for the further purpose of making of the Declaration of Independence something more than the mere form of words that it has thus far been. For such interposition their State stands fully qualified, her record being as bright and as free from any taint of selfishness as that of any other community whose history has been recorded. She has not now, nor has she ever had, any interest that is not common to twenty other States. Never has SHE abandoned her friends.* Never has she made demand for anything to be enjoyed by herself alone. In regard to the production of iron she stands now as far above all other States as does your State in regard to cottons, yet does she insist on that perfect protection which must aid in development of the wonderful mineral resources of the country from the Lakes to the Gulf, and from the Atlantic to the Pacific. For herself, therefore, she asks nothing. For the Union she asks, and will insist upon, that harmony and peace which must result from proper appreciation of the fact, that while it is quite in the power of the Producing States to change their places of exchange and their agents, it is not in the power of the Trading States to find elsewhere such patient milch-cows as they have thus far proved themselves to be. To make the demand therefor has now become her duty, and so great has become the dissatisfaction—I might use a stronger word—at the extreme selfishness of eastern friends, that were the question of its performance now submitted to a vote, it would command the assent of four out of five of the whole people of the State.

· Might not, you may ask, a movement like that I have indicated, lead to another civil war? Certainly not. To the great natural resources of the hill and mountain country was the South·indebted for power to maintain the recent war. To the more developed resources of the mountain country of the North have we stood indebted for power to extinguish the rebellion. When the whole mountain region shall be of one mind it will be found that the people of the flats can make no war. As Pennsylvania has gone so has always gone the Union. As she now goes, so will it go. She does now go for abolition of monopolies, Northern, Eastern, and British, and it may be well for our Republican friends of the trading States to know that the days of their existence have been already counted, and have been found to be very few in number.

Ten years since, after the occurrence of the great financial crisis

[From the "Globe," Feb. 24, 1855.]

* "The manufacturers of Massachusetts were willing to assent to a reduction of manufactured articles for the reason *that it was accompanied by a still greater reduction* on raw material. * * * *

"The way to break down protection is to strike at it in detail; by detaching from its support interests that are willing to be detached."—Mr. BANKS, of Massachusetts.

"When, sir, the effort was made to detach the Pennsylvania representatives by appeals to their peculiar interests, what did you see? When we were told that ample protection would be given to the iron interest if we would strike a fatal blow at the interests of other States, the united delegation from Pennsylvania, Whigs and Democrats, answered: No!"—Mr. HOWE, of Pennsylvania.

of 1857, but in advance of his first message, I addressed Mr. Buchanan a private letter in which he was told that persistence in the policy of his predecessor would result in his own ruin and that of his party, and in dissolution of the Union. Of course he did not believe of this even a single word, it being a rule with our public men never to believe in anything until too late. That letter is, however, a tolerable history of what has since occurred. Now, my dear sir, I do the same by you. You, as I fear, will do as Mr. Buchanan did, not believing what has been predicted. Within the next decade those predictions will have become history, and your fellow-citizens may then find reason to regret that, like Mr. Buchanan, you had not believed, until *too late.*

Begging you to excuse my repeated trespasses on your kind attention, I remain, with great regard,

Yours truly,

HENRY C. CAREY.

Hon. H. Wilson.

Philadelphia, September 30, 1867.

POSTSCRIPT.

Since writing the above I find the following in the *New York Times:*—

THE REPUBLICAN PARTY—ITS GREATEST PERIL.

The warning of the Maine election came not a moment too soon for the welfare of the Republican party. The West furnishes abundant indications of the danger it encounters as a consequence of the determination of cliques and factions to foist upon it issues quite foreign to the recognized objects of its organization. Senator Grimes's vigorous protest against the attempt to make the prohibitory tariff a test of party orthodoxy, receives the indorsement of the leading Republicans of his State. Gen. Baker, Adjutant-General, and one of its most influential men, writes "that if the tariff lobby succeed in interpolating into the creed of the Republican party a prohibitory tariff plank, and making that the issue, the Republican party of the Northwest will be smashed to atoms." Strong as the statement is, we are persuaded that it does not transcend the truth. Throughout the Northwest the Republican press is unanimous in its denunciation of the combinations which try to manipulate the action of Congress on the tariff question; admitting the necessity of high duties in existing circumstances, but resisting any assertion of the prohibitory principle in the interest of classes.

History is constantly repeating itself. The above is but a new edition of the advice given to the party in 1860, and given by all the British free trade journals, the *Times* included. How it was then answered by the Convention we all now know, and my readers have been informed as to the reasons why the answer had been such as secured the election of Mr. Lincoln.

For a present answer I beg to offer the following paragraphs from the London correspondence of the same *New York Times*, just two days later in date :—

"The correspondents of English papers give melancholy accounts of dull business in commerce and manufactures in America; but the remedy for this is so easy, as pointed out in a *Times* leader, that it is only necessary to call an extra session of Congress and adopt it. You have only to remove all restrictions upon Free Trade. Repeal all duties upon imports, and every ship-yard would be alive with workers, every factory in full operation, and the whole country prosperous and happy. But the trouble is that nobody in America knows anything about political economy. Under the actual tariff, it is said that American manufacturers are undersold by those of England and Germany—a Free Trade would bring all right again. It happens, however, that England, with Free Trade, is scarcely building any ships, and that she is in serious danger from Continental competition. How is this muddle to be disposed of? With Free Trade, half the laboring population in England lives upon wages just above the point of starvation, with no resource in sickness or old age but the workhouse, and Ireland is in a state of chronic poverty and discontent. With Free Trade, there is a perpetual war between capital and labor, and the enormous burden of pauperism is increasing. Americans may be ignorant of political economy, but I cannot see that the English are overburdened with wisdom, or that the practical results of their system are of a very enticing character. The workingmen of England believe in protection, and the English colonies practice it, to the great annoyance of the theorists at home.

"After all, Free Trade is a proved impossibility. Parliament is constantly interfering with what, according to our philosophers, should regulate itself. The Poor Law system is itself a protective measure. So are all the laws limiting the hours and ages, and regulating the conditions of labor. We have acts of Parliament forbidding the employment of women in coal-pits, where, a few years ago, they worked naked like brute beasts; acts forbidding the employment in factories of children of twelve years; and, during the last session, laws have been passed for the protection of children in the numerous trades and in the agricultural gangs which would disgrace Dahomey. There is need of abundance more of such interference. In the black country, north of Birmingham, there is a large population engaged in making nails by hand labor—especially horse-shoe nails. On an average, three females are employed in this work to one male. I wonder if, in all America, there is one female blacksmith. Even the strongest-minded of the advocates of woman's rights have not claimed for women the trade of a blacksmith. But here little girls from seven to nine years old are set to work, and kept at work as long as they can stand, hammering at the anvil, roasting by the forge, blacked with soot, never seeing school-house or play-ground, but employed their whole lives making horse-shoe nails for a bare subsistence. Absolute Free Trade sets women and children to work at forge and mine and reduces wages to the lowest possible standard; and that is the system against which humanity protests, and with which Parliament, in spite of theories, finds it necessary to interfere. Free Trade, as ultimated in England, is the most debased ignorance, the most abhorrent cruelty, the most disgusting vice, and the most heart-breaking misery, that can be seen in any country, calling itself civilized and Christian."

RESUMPTION No. 1.

In his first report to Congress, December, 1865, Mr. Secretary McCullough told that body that the currency was in excess, and that prices were too high ; that the former must be contracted and the latter reduced ; that the debt was burdensome and dangerous, and needed to be paid ; and that, to the end that he might be enabled so rapidly to proceed in the work of payment as to complete it within thirty years, he desired to have appropriated to the discharge of principal and payment of interest an annual amount of $200,000,000. That done, he was of opinion that the day of resumption would prove to be not far distant.

In his second report (December, 1866), after expressing great regret that Congress should, so far as regarded the non-interest-bearing portion of the debt, have limited his contractive powers to $4,000,000 per month, and that he should thus have been "prevented from taking the first important step towards a return to specie payments," he urged that for the present fiscal year his powers should be so extended as to enable him to cancel circulating notes at the rate of $6,000,000 per month, and thereafter at the rate of $10,000,000 per month until the whole should have been extinguished. These things done, he believed that we should be ready for resumption in July, 1868, if not even "at a still earlier day."

The views thus presented had previously been given to the world in his Fort Wayne speech, made more than two years since. Throughout those years every effort has been made to put a stop to exchanges of property for labor. From day to day the world has been assured that prices were yet quite too high ; that they must and would fall ; that those who now built ships or houses, furnaces or factories, would find that they had given for them far more than they then were worth ; and thus has the sword of Damocles been held suspended over the heads of our people until a paralysis has been produced that is scarcely less complete than were those which accompanied the financial crisis of 1837 and 1857. Purchases are now made only from day to day, or from hour to hour, none desiring to be caught with merchandise on hand when the day of final settlement shall have been reached. Prices fall steadily, but the lower the price the stronger is the belief that there is yet before us a still lower deep, and the more the desire to refrain from supplying even the most necessary wants until the lowest deep shall have been arrived at. Threats of early resumption having brought us to this sad condition, it is now, in sheer despair, suggested that we should almost at once take the great leap, making public declaration that at an early day the Treasury would be prepared to redeem with gold its obligations of any and every kind, and that from and after that day the banks would be required, on pain of forfeiture of their charters, to do the same. The Rubicon would then have been passed ; the lowest point would then have been reached ; men would then begin again to buy and sell ; commerce would then become active ; mills and furnaces would then be built; and prosperity would then again become the order of the day. So, at least, we are assured by those journals which advocate the Secretary's policy, and most especially by some of those of New York and New England.

The proverb, however, advises that you look before you leap, and that is what, for the benefit of our readers, we propose now to do, presenting for their consideration, to the best of our ability, an exact statement of the position at which, at the close of the second year of the contractive policy, we have arrived, and leaving to them then to judge for themselves how far it would be expedient to take the extraordinary leap that, in accordance with all the past teaching of the Secretary and his friends, is thus proposed.

The public debt is now, in round numbers, $2,500,000,000. Of this only $2,100,000,000 as yet bear interest, but to that amount there should this year be added $72,000,000, and next year $120,000,000, until at length in 1870 the whole should draw interest payable in gold, and making demands upon the Treasury to the annual extent of $150,000,000. The present demand, admitting that resumption had now taken place, would be but $126,000,000, but to this would have to be added diplomatic expenses, maintenance of fleets abroad, and payment for Walrussia, Samana, and other territories that have been or may be purchased, the whole making little if any less than $140,000,000, to be gradually increased until it shall reach $155,000,000, if not even $160,000,000.

For obtaining the gold thus needed the Treasury is now wholly dependent on receipts from customs duties, the average of which, as shown by the Treasury report, but little exceeds forty per cent. To enable us to receive from that source the sum of $140,000,000, we need to import foreign merchandise to the declared extent of nearly $350,000,000.

To this must now be added a sum sufficient to cover the under valuations, the smuggling, and the passengers' baggage, this last alone amounting to very many millions. By many, ourselves included, it is believed that these involve an additional hundred millions, but we shall content ourselves with taking them at only $60,000,000, giving $410,000,000 as the annual amount of merchandise that must be imported to enable the Treasury to obtain from that source the gold required for enabling it to meet the gold demands upon it.

Nearly the whole of our intercourse with Europe, and very much of it with the rest of the world, being now maintained by means of foreign ships, we need now to add to the above, for freights and passage money, not less than $10,000,000. It may be twice that amount, but we are content to place it at the one we thus have named, giving so far a total of $420,000,000.

To this must be added the expenses of our absentees, travelling and resident, sometimes estimated at $100,000,000. We, however, are satisfied to place them at $60,000,000, by adding which to the amount above given, we obtain as payable abroad, $480,000,000.

Adding next for dividends on stocks held abroad, and for interest on public and private debts, only $60,000,000, we obtain a total of $540,000,000 payable in foreign countries, and in gold. How is this vast demand to be met? Let us see!

Exclusive of gold and cotton, our exports, valued in greenbacks, for the fiscal year 1866, amounted to $189,000,000
For the second half of the present fiscal year they
   were $83,000,000. Taking the same amount for
   the first half, we have a total of   166,000,000
It is little likely that those of the present year will be
   greater, but we are content to estimate them at   190,000,000

Contraction having closed many of our cotton mills, while forcing very many of them to work short time, the domestic demand for the raw material has so far declined that the price has fallen to less than 18 cents, or about $80 per bale of 450 pounds.

Of the last crop we exported 1,216,000 bales, yielding, probably, little short of $200,000,000. The present one, as now reported by the Bureau of Statistics, will give but 1,568,000 bales, of which we should retain, even with the present diminished consumption, 650,000. This would leave less than 1,000,000 for export, giving $80,000,000 as the amount to be added to the miscellaneous list, and making our total exports, gold excepted, $270,000,000.

Converting this into gold, we obtain less than $190,000,000 with which to meet demands that, as has been shown, exceed $500,000,-000.* For the balance we *must* give either gold or bonds. As regards the first, however, the same influences are at work to prevent extension of mining operations throughout the centre, the west, and the south. Paralysis forces capital back to the commercial cities, and gold mines remain unworked that under a different system would even now be yielding tens of millions. Coal and cotton, gold and iron, feel thus alike the benumbing effects of a policy that to us appears the most vicious that has ever been proposed by any finance minister the world as yet has seen.

Under such circumstances, what would be the value of a declaration on the part of the Treasury of its ability to resume payment in specie of its obligations? Would any sane man believe that it could do so for even a single week? If none such could or would do so, could resumption have any effect other than that of distributing among private hoards the gold now hoarded in

---

* It is positively asserted that the report above referred to is wholly incorrect, and that the cotton crop will exceed 2,000,000. Should this prove to be the case, the addition in gold to be made to our exports may be $25,000,000, giving a total of $215,000,000.

Treasury vaults ? That done, to what quarter would the Secretary look for means with which to meet demands for interest ?

This question is submitted in the hope that some of those who now so strongly advocate the Secretary's policy may be induced to explain how it is that, in their belief, resumption may be first attained and then maintained.　　　　　　　　　　　　C.

RESUMPTION No. 2.

The Secretary's friends seem unwilling to exhibit the process by means of which, in their belief, resumption may be either attained or maintained. They do not explain how it is to be—the age of miracles being supposed to have passed away—that, in the face of an annual deficit in our transactions with foreigners which now counts by hundreds of millions, and that grows with each successive year, we are to be enabled to retain among ourselves the produce of our mines with a view to resumption of the use of the precious metals. They have little relish for calculations other than those furnished by the Treasury, no two of which seem to be much in harmony with each other. They shriek "resumption," at the same time threatening that if the legislative authority shall in any manner interfere with the Secretary's plans, "the movement will be delayed at least by Executive interposition." It is thus threatened that if Congress shall, as it certainly must, arrive at the conclusion that continuance in the policy of contraction can have no result other than that of repudiation, the President will interpose his veto, in the hope and belief, as we suppose, that he may be thus enabled to succeed in placing the loyal and the rebel debts on a level with each other. To accomplish this would certainly please him much, and none are laboring more to gratify him than are those professed friends of resumption, and professed opponents of Executive usurpation, by whom this threat has but now been uttered. How far Congress will find itself disposed to afford him such gratification we have yet to see.

The New England States, as represented in Congress, are urgent for an early return to specie payments. Why? Because, with little more than *a twelfth* of the population, they have secured to themselves more than *a third* of the great money monopoly that, under the new banking law, has been created! Because, to those States, small as they are, there has been granted an average circulation of no less than seventeen millions! Because, the large amount of capital that has been there allowed to be invested in banking prevents necessity for the over-trading that exists in the less favored States of the centre, the south, and the west! Because the channels of commerce are there so abundantly filled with notes of every size as almost to annihilate demand for either legal tender notes or the precious metals! Because, but very few millions would suffice for supplying all their needs; and because those millions would, on the day of resumption, be at once obtained from Treasury vaults! Because, being creditor States, they desire that all existing claims shall be paid in gold, the commodity of highest value! Because, being purchasers of wool, cotton, and other raw material, they desire that the agricultural and mining States may find themselves compelled to accept the lowest prices! For all these reasons the votes of eastern members are almost unanimously favorable to the Treasury policy of contraction.

Equally unanimous in their opposition to it are the people occupying the vast Territory south of the Delaware and the Ohio and west of the Mississippi, fifteen millions in number, and likely soon to be thirty millions. Why? Because, to their thirty States and territories, with *two-fifths* of our total population, there has been allotted but a *ninth* of the great money monopoly that now exists. Because, while the average circulation allotted to the little New England States is more than $17,000,000, that allotted to their States and Territories scarcely exceeds a single million! Because, by reason of the monopoly that has been created they now find themselves almost entirely dependent on legal tenders for machinery of circulation! Because, to give them gold by means of which they should be placed upon an equal footing with the highly favored eastern States, would require more than thrice the quantity now in Treasury vaults! Because, even now, they gladly pay from two to five per cent. per month for the use of circulating notes issued by eastern banks, for the private profit of their stockholders! Because, with every step in the progress of contraction, the price of money tends to rise, and that of wool or cotton tends to fall! Because, even now they find themselves ground as between the upper and the nether millstone! Because, being debtor States, they prefer to pay in the commodity that was receivable at the date of contraction of the debt! Because, being sellers of raw products, they do not desire to be thrown on the "tender mercies" of eastern traders, leaving to them to fix the prices at which they will receive those products. For all these reasons the people of two-thirds of the States and territories of the Union, rightly believing that the Treasury policy can have no result other than that of making them mere hewers of wood and drawers of water to their more favored brethren of the east and north, are to a man opposed to it.

Before the war, with a banking capital of 85 millions, the New England States had a circulation of 34 millions. To-day, with 145 of the one, they have 103 of the other—this latter having more than trebled in the short space of seven years Thus well provided at home, they find themselves ready to dispense with Treasury notes.

With an almost equal population and almost equally engaged in other than agricultural pursuits, Pennsylvania's share in the great money monopoly is but little more than a third as great, whether as regards either capital or circulation. Therefore is it that she is more dependent on the use of Treasury credit, and quite determined to resist the policy of contraction.

Before the war, Georgia had 16,000,000 of capital and half that amount of circulation. To-day, she is most graciously allowed to have two of the one and one of the other.

Before the war, Missouri had nine of capital and eight of circulation. To-day, greatly growing as she is, she is most kindly permitted to have four of the former and two of the latter. Need we then wonder that her people, as well as those of Georgia, see in the Treasury policy nothing but absolute subjection to the will of eastern capitalists and utter ruin to themselves? Most extra-ordinary would it be did they fail so to do!

The tendency towards resumption thus exists in the precise ratio of the presence of those substitutes for the precious metals which almost annihilate the demand for gold. On the other hand, the opposition to it exists in the direct ratio of such absence of those substitutes as makes those metals the almost exclusive medium of circulation. Such being the case, the road towards specie payments would seem to lie in the direction of placing the centre, the south, and the west as nearly as possible in the same position with the eastern States, giving them notes of every denomination, and thereby lessening the demand for gold. Directly the reverse of this, however, the Secretary insists that they shall now surrender the legal tender notes, and make almost exclusive use of gold and silver. Whence, however, are these to come? Paralysis, caused by Treasury action, forbids development of their mining interests, and mines remain unworked that, under other circumstances, would furnish the supplies that are now so greatly needed. Thus is it that the Secretary is busily engaged in burning the candle at both ends, diminishing the supply of the very commodity by means of which, almost alone, he insists that the people of those numerous States and territories shall make exchanges of food for labor, of labor for cotton, cloth and iron. This *may* be the road towards resumption, but to us it seems more like that which finds its end in repudiation.

Study the Secretary's policy where we may, we obtain the same results. The seven-thirties make no demand for gold. Compound interest notes make none. Legal-tenders make none. That they may be enabled so to do, it is needed that the form of debt be changed, and that gold-bearing certificates, fitted for exportation, be issued in their stead.

That is the work on which the Secretary is now engaged, his whole energies being given to the manufacture of bonds for European markets. With each successive bond exported there arises a new demand for gold with which to pay abroad the interest. With each there is increased facility for importing cloth and iron that should be made at home. With each there is increased demand for gold with which to pay the duties. With each there is a diminution in the product of oil and cotton sent to distant markets.

In all times past it has been held that the road towards resumption lay in the direction of diminishing demand for the precious metals, while increasing the supply thereof. All this, however, is to be now unlearned, the Secretary having discovered that the more the supply can be diminished and the demand increased, the sooner shall we attain the much-desired end. It may be that it will thus be reached, but if it shall be so, there will thus be furnished conclusive evidence that the age of miracles has returned.

C.

[From the National American.]

INDUSTRIAL RECONSTRUCTION OF THE SOUTH.

LOUISIANA held its first grand State fair under conduct of the Mechanics and Agricultural Fair Association, on the 26th November, 1866. We have the report of its proceedings, including premium essays and addresses, and have read it with unmingled pleasure, not unfrequently heightened by surprise. One of the orators goes at large into what he styles "The causes which led to southern subjugation; and the means by which the South may be restored to prosperity and power." On a rapid examination of statements and arguments, we find nothing said and nothing omitted that a picked representative of northern opinions could improve. He traces the conquest of the South to the superior economic policy of the North—to the difference of the industries of the two sections, from which resulted all the difference of power to make and maintain the war. The hope of restoration he necessarily puts upon the frank acceptance of her situation by the South, and such change of industrial and commercial policy as shall make her self-supplying and self-supporting. In a word, she must diversify her productions, agricultural and manufacturing, after the model of the Northern States; and she must educate her whole people, white and black, rich and poor, up to the point of qualifying them all for their respective functions in society. Moreover, she must actively encourage the immigration of foreign mechanics and mariners, with the double purpose of making her own manufactures, and securing the domination of the white race in the social and political systems. Of which last-named motive we need say nothing, for we care nothing about a side issue of this sort. Only let them do the right things, and then the things will take care of themselves, and of their political and social issues.

Altogether, it is with uncommon pleasure that we find these people growing wise, as well as earnest, in reconstructing themselves. Among the essays read at this Fair is a very brief one on "Raising Swine in Louisiana," by Judge Robertson, whose remarkable report upon the resources of Louisiana, made to the Legislature in January last, may have come under the notice of some of our readers.

The points made by the Judge are substantially these : owing to the difference of climate hogs are at least doubly more prolific in Louisiana than in Ohio or Illinois; always producing two litters in the year against one in the colder North, and bringing them to maturity with great certainty. Owing to the same cause they need no housing in the winter, and can find roots and grasses, green and fresh, for pasturage all the year. The average yield of the sweet potato there is 200 bushels to the acre, and twice as many can be raised. This root is found to make pork equally as fast as the like weight of corn ; giving an average of 200 to the potato against an average of thirty bushels of corn, as the yield of food ; the culture of the former being at the same time much less expensive than of the latter. Barley there averages fifty bushels to the acre, while at the North and West it is but little over twenty ; it is far superior to corn in giving body and frame to the hog, and it comes so early in the season that it may be used in raising the young pigs, and preparing the stock for fattening. Louisiana produces, besides potatoes and barley for hog feed, a semitropical abundance of peas, pumpkins, peanuts, squashes, peaches (!) and Jerusalem artichokes. The Judge concludes by saying that he believes hog raising to be far more profitable for that region than either cotton or sugar planting ; that they have every advantage over the Northwest in the competition ; that they have salt better and cheaper ; that their hams and bacon are equal to any in the Union ; that they abound in the woods used for packing ; and, being situated at the mouth of the Mississippi, they have the immense advantage of a short and cheap inland transportation ; and, finally, that they can and will supply the world's markets with this great article of export.

It is really pleasant to the head and heart of a sound political economist to see the South thus turning her back upon the causes of all her troubles, and setting the example to the Northwest of a sound and healthy system of industrial enterprise ; entering upon a course of diversified production which, of itself, will compel the Northwest to adopt a like progressive and secure economic policy. Cotton having lost its provinces, corn will be obliged to live at home. For both, the system of hazardous dependence upon distant regions is broken up forever. Let all parties take notice and prepare.